MW01611668

HOW TO FIND LAND FOR TINY HOUSE LIVING

TINY HOME BUDGETING AND FINANCIALS, REAL ESTATE, ZONING, AND CODE

JORDAN LIBERATA

TINYHOUSEPRACTICAL.COM

CONTENTS

A HELPFUL TOOL FOR YOUR SUCCESS...

The supplemental **Tiny House Quickstarter** provides a tiny house checklist, a budgeting tool, a location tracker, and a list of must-avoid mistakes most people don't know they're making. Get yours now by going to my website!

Scan the QR code below!

jordanliberata.com

INTRODUCTION

A recent survey of aspiring tiny house owners asked, "what is your biggest tiny house challenge?"

35% said that finding land and navigating zoning is their top challenge, while 26% said that money is the most difficult barrier.

Many new to the tiny house movement may see these numbers and ask, *are you telling me that building the tiny house isn't the most complex part?*

Yes, that is exactly what I'm telling you.

The reality is that the challenge in a tiny house is not so much the design or even the construction but the placement and affordability of it. This situation can be pretty painful for aspiring tiny house owners because freedom—financial and otherwise—is one of the main drivers behind tiny house living.

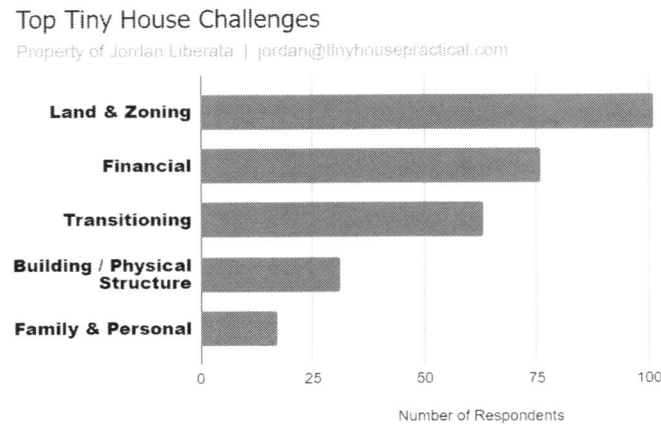

Top Tiny House Challenges

Property of Jordan Liberata | jordan@tinyhousepractical.com

If you are reading this book, chances are you are somewhat familiar, or perhaps all too familiar, with this reality. You may have spent a lot of time designing your tiny house, only to realize that making that perfect design a reality seems impossible. Maybe you have started running the numbers and have no idea how you will afford this, or perhaps you find the whole world of zoning and permitting so confusing you don't know how you will possibly overcome it.

I'm here to tell you that you can overcome these barriers, and this book will teach you how.

In my years involved in the tiny house movement, I've spent time writing books and articles about practical ways to approach the tiny house lifestyle and have interacted with thousands of aspiring and existing tiny house owners. I've always been a proponent of tiny houses as a means to an end: that tiny houses are not the goal but rather the tool to achieving a goal. For many, that goal is financial freedom. For others, it is connecting with nature and seeking adventure or purpose. For some, it is minimalism and environmental consciousness. For me personally, it is all of the above. In my time spent in tiny houses and off-grid, I've always found an incredible simplicity and sense of freedom. Yet I realized, through my interactions with those wishing to live tiny, that attaining this freedom is incredibly challenging, so I set out to solve this problem. That is why I spent hundreds of hours researching solutions to this problem and learning the approaches of tiny house owners and real estate developers alike. If they can do it, so can we, right?

This book is the first of its kind. You can certainly find lots of tiny house content on design and construction and the basics of tiny living. I have written a tiny house beginners book and a tiny house on wheels construction book for those that are just getting started or seeking to understand construction. But until now, no book has tackled this all-consuming and all-important question: *how do I find the location and money for my tiny house, and how do I navigate the zoning and code that applies specifically to me?* This book will answer this question, telling you what you need to do and how you need to do it.

Let's get this out on the table now: this process is not easy. If it were, this book wouldn't exist. But it is attainable and doable without draining your bank account, and it is not nearly as out of reach as many people fear. Whether you want to buy a tiny house for your retirement or build a tiny house as a second home, whether you are striving for financial freedom or seeking adventure, whether you want a minimalist lifestyle, an off-grid lifestyle, or neither, fear not! You have come to the right place.

Ultimately, if you are someone who wants to unpack the financials behind buying or building a tiny house, who wants to know how to reduce the financial risk of a tiny house, who wants to figure out how to navigate zoning and building codes, who wants to learn the secrets to finding and buying land, and who wants to understand the process from start to finish, this book is for you. If nothing else, this book will shed light on the process of turning a tiny house idea into a tiny house reality, so you know which parts of the process you need to outsource and which elements you can do yourself.

You won't find pretty pictures of tiny houses in this book, nor will you find opinions about what is and isn't right about how the world treats tiny houses. Everything in this book is about practicality, focused on equipping you with the proper strategies and mindset to afford and properly place your tiny home.

If you're nervous or overwhelmed by these topics, it is ok. We've all been there. Think of this book as your roadmap and your toolbox. Think of it as your motivational coach and guide. By the end of it, you will understand financials, land, zoning, and code. You will know just about all you need to know so that you can go into the process with your eyes wide open.

If you want to go on this ride with me, know that you *can* do it. And if you want it bad enough, know that you *will* make your tiny house dream a reality. Let's get to work.

FUNDAMENTALS

Before we explore the details of financials, zoning, tiny house real estate, or building codes, we must first consider how all of these topics are related and get a sense of the overall who, what, when, and where of our endeavor.

Within this chapter, we will introduce ourselves to the overall process, so you know what to expect in this book. Next, we will cover the people involved, the misconceptions you need to get straight, and the basics of zoning and building codes.

Let's dive in!

TINY HOUSE PROCESS

The overall process outlined here is also that which will be covered throughout this book in more detail, but it is key that you understand everything that is involved and the general order of the events. With that said, know that the process of moving from "I want a tiny house" to "I live in a tiny house" is dynamic; it has many steps that are intertwined, and you will likely have to bounce back and forth between steps. This non-linear journey is the reality of finding land for a non-traditional structure. In fact, it is the reality of finding land in general.

Accept that this will be challenging at times, but also understand that patience, positivity, and determination —along with the guidance you receive in this book— will get you to your goal.

Now that we've ripped off that band-aid, let's walk through the overall process.

Step 1: Make a Plan

Congrats, you are already making a plan by reading this book! When it comes to tiny houses, you must always have a *measure twice, cut once* mentality. That means doing thorough and focused planning before starting, whether it is the budgeting process, the design of your house, the process of finding land, the process of getting permits, or the construction itself. Making a plan ultimately results in less time, less money, and less risk.

Step 2: Find Land & Identify Zoning

As we will cover extensively, your first action after the planning and budgeting process will be finding the land itself. This search will start with a broad area comprising several counties, municipalities, towns, or even states or provinces.

Once you have identified the land, you will need to identify specific parcels within those areas and the zoning ordinances that apply. We will get to this in much more detail.

Next comes narrowing down the specific parcels of land to those you are serious about buying, discussing your plans with the local zoning department and likely the planning or building department, and then moving forward with your purchase of the land.

To buy the land, you will need to make an offer and negotiate with the seller. This stage is also the time when financing will come into play. Once the loan is approved, the property may then be appraised, a lawyer might review the contracts, and then you will close on the land purchase.

If you are not buying land and are simply renting, you will go through a less rigorous process that also includes research and due diligence. We will cover that in Chapter 3.

Step 3: Submit Plans to Local Department(s) & Get Permits

Even though you will already have gotten informal approval from local zoning and planning boards, you will now need to submit your plans formally. This process will mean getting any special permits that are required based on the zoning rules, as well as building permits for the construction itself. The latter will likely require you to submit your design plans.

After submitting, you may be asked to adjust your plans based on the ordinance and code. At that point, you will make corrections, resubmit, and receive your permits.

Step 4: Build the Tiny House

If you are constructing the house yourself, you will now legally be able to do so. If you bought your tiny house, you can have it delivered.

Step 5: Final Inspection & Certification of Occupancy

The final step is to have your tiny house inspected and receive your certification of occupancy from your local zoning or building department. This is essentially the form affirming that you can legally live in the space.

THINK IT THROUGH

The number one piece of advice that aspiring tiny house owners often overlook is to understand why they want a tiny house in the first place. While most people have a sense of why they want to go tiny, many don't dig much deeper than that.

There are many reasons to live in a tiny house, whether permanently, temporarily, or as a vacation home. The top reasons are financial freedom, adventure, minimalism, connection with nature, sustainability, and retirement. Typically, the tiny house is not the goal but the means of achieving the goal.

Whatever your reason for living tiny, make sure you always base your decisions on that motivation. It is surprisingly easy to lose sight of why you want a tiny house, and instead focus all of your attention on getting a tiny house, but if the tiny house is merely a tool, you might be sacrificing the wrong things in your pursuits. For example, if you are seeking a tiny house for connection with nature but end up with a tiny house in a crowded area, you have not reached the intended goal even though you have a tiny house.

Secondly, the motive for living in a tiny home dictates the land you need and the type of tiny house you build or buy.

If you are seeking privacy and simplicity, you likely want private and secluded land and could be happy with a tiny house on wheels or a tiny house on a foundation.

If you need your home to be mobile, then the land will be less important than the tiny house on wheels.

If you want to be a part of a community, you will want to find a tiny house village or simply a place close to other people in a vibrant and like-minded community setting.

If you require a tiny house for a senior to live independently but close to caregivers or loved ones, you need to seek land that is zoned for an accessory dwelling unit, also known as an ADU.

The examples go on.

Going through this exercise may seem unnecessary, but it will help you and your family identify what you can and cannot compromise, as finding a place for your tiny house will likely require some sacrifice.

KEY PEOPLE INVOLVED

There are many people and entities that you will deal with throughout the process, each with different roles and different motives. Understand both, and you will be able to partner with them appropriately.

Seller of the Land

An individual or a bank may sell the land that you are looking to buy. For both, the goal is simple: sell the land at as high a price as possible or as quickly as possible, or both. Some individuals may have other requirements too. For example, you may find someone looking to sell land that has been in their family for five generations. In this case, that person likely has an emotional tie to the land and may care about what you plan to do with the land.

Regardless, make sure that you know the motivations of the seller. You don't need to like the person selling you the land, but it helps to approach them—and everyone else in the process—with friendly positivity and an internal mindset of healthy skepticism.

Sellers often expect cash payments. While you may be able to negotiate seller financing, know that the land business is a cash-first business.

Lenders

You may deal with lenders both for the land and the tiny house itself. Understand that both are different from typical mortgage lenders. In all cases, a lender's goal is to minimize their financial risk. Unfortunately, both tiny houses and land are considered riskier than traditional homes.

Tiny houses rarely receive mortgages and instead are financed through personal loans or seller financing, meaning you are more likely to need to dish out a down payment of 20-30%.

Land does not get mortgaged. In the eyes of a lender, land is considered a riskier investment, especially if your plans for the land are unorthodox or complex, such as building a tiny home. For this reason, expect to put down 40-60% for a land loan.

Ultimately, reputable lenders are fair. They think in terms of math and risk, and they want you to be able to make your purchase because it means they will earn income. The key here is to ensure that you are, in fact, working with a reputable lender, such as a bank with which you already have a relationship.

Zoning Departments

The zoning department of the county, city, province, or town that you ultimately choose will play a big part in your process. They can make your project a nightmare, or they can make it easy-breezy. Luckily, this relationship is largely in your control.

Zoning departments are comprised of people whose job is to determine the way that land is used, which is what we call a zoning ordinance. Additionally, their job is to ensure that people follow the zoning ordinance and help them comply with it. That last part is important: *their job is to* **help**.

Because of the challenges of zoning in many countries, especially the United States, zoning as a concept has a bad reputation. Now I'm not here to debate the positives or shortcomings of zoning because that is a complex topic and has no practical benefit. What *is* practical is understanding that while zoning as an institution is overcomplicated and perhaps dysfunctional, zoning departments typically consist of friendly people who usually want to help you.

Befriend them. Call them early in the process. Lean on them. It will pay off.

Neighbors

Neighbors could play a significant role in your tiny house life, not so much in the beginning, but once you are already there.

I recently spoke with a tiny house owner who had been living in her tiny house in rural New England for a few years. She hadn't gone through the process of properly getting approval from the zoning department, which was not an issue...until it was. One day, an inspector showed up, and the zoning department issued her an order to leave her land, which she then had to fight in a process that lasted over a year.

The zoning department did not initiate this inspection. It was initiated by a neighbor who didn't like how her tiny house looked. The vast majority of zoning departments operate this way. They only take action when there is a complaint, and complaints almost always come from neighbors.

Get to know your neighbors. Talk to them about your tiny house. Hear their concerns and come up with solutions together if possible. Sometimes your solution can be as simple as planting some bushes that hide your trailer wheels, installing a fence, or simply having a conversation to make your neighbor feel heard.

Building/Planning Departments

Like the zoning department, the building or planning department plays a specific role in a community. Their job is to ensure that structures on the land are safe. That often means ensuring that the structures are built to code and that the systems on the property do not violate land-related codes, such as water rights.

You will likely deal with this department when it comes time to get approval for your build plans. Like the zoning department, you should partner with this group instead of ignoring or circumventing them.

Inspectors

Inspectors are often an extension of the building or zoning department, and their goal is to ensure that the land and structure are up to code.

You can expect to see inspectors when you start your build and certainly when you finish it. You may even see them during the process.

If you go the under the radar route, you may see them once you live in your tiny house.

Inspectors can be a mixed bag. Most are reasonable, but some are sticklers. Be friendly with them, answer their questions, have your construction documentation prepared, and don't overshare. Even though you should do everything to code and ordinance, divulging a ton of information opens up rabbit holes. Most of the time, the inspector doesn't even want to go there themselves.

Contractors

Contractors can be general contractors, electricians, plumbers, manufacturers, or anyone that does skilled labor for you.

A general rule of thumb with contractors is to get multiple quotes and references. If the contractor can't provide references, they are not reputable. Way too many people have shared stories of getting scammed out of tens of thousands of dollars. Do your due diligence.

Additionally, make sure that they have tiny house construction experience. Tiny house construction has some nuance that is different from traditional homes.

Tiny House Resellers

Many markets exist for people to sell their tiny homes, which can be an excellent option for you. However, tiny house purchases are like car purchases: *buyer beware*.

You should understand not only how the tiny house looks but also how it is built. Additionally, understand that tiny houses tend to depreciate with time, similar to a car, so if someone built a tiny house for $40,000, lived in it for five years, and is now trying to sell it to you for $50,000, the tiny house is most likely overpriced. It should be more in the $20,000-$30,000 range.

Real Estate Agent or Broker

Throughout this book, we will use the term *real estate agent* to refer to a real estate agent or broker. You will also hear the term realtor, which is sometimes slightly different. Here is what you need to know about each:

- **Real Estate Agent**: A real estate agent represents a buyer or seller in the process of a property sale. Real estate agents work for real estate agencies, also known as real estate brokerages.
- **Real Estate Broker:** A real estate broker is a real estate agent that continues their education and receives a license to be a broker. A broker can start their own real estate brokerage or work independently of a brokerage. Some brokers still choose to work for a brokerage.
- **Realtor:** A realtor is a general term that refers to someone who has a clean track record, a real estate license, is actively engaged in the real estate industry, and has paid to be a member of the National Association of Realtors (at least in the United States). Not all realtors are real

estate agents or brokers. They can also be appraisers, salespeople, property managers, or anyone who meets the above criteria.

To find the land you need, a real estate agent or broker will suffice. Ultimately, they are there to help you successfully purchase the land. They are professionals at finding land and navigating the complexities of land purchase. They are a solid resource that may have connections with the local zoning and building departments and perhaps lawyers and architects.

Real estate agents typically take a 5-10% commission on the sale. There may be a real estate agent involved that represents you, known as the *buyer's agent*, as well as one that represents the seller, known as the *listing agent*. In this case, the commission is split between the two agents. Nevertheless, in most cases, the seller of the land pays the whole commission. When this is the case, using an agent is not much of a downside. However, it is critical to understand that real estate agents of all kinds are paid commissions and thus incentivized to get you to buy. This reality doesn't mean they are sleazy and dishonest, but you should take what they say with a grain of salt. You should also not lean on them too heavily when addressing critical topics, such as zoning.

In the unlikely event that you will have to pay your agent, understand that it may be worthwhile. If you buy land for $50,000 and must pay 5% at close, you are still only paying $2,500. Compare this to the cost of hiring a lawyer, not to mention the risk associated with navigating murky waters alone; this amount of money may be well worth it. Ideally, you find a property where you don't have to deal with this unusual commission structure.

Lastly, it is possible to have an agent that is both a listing agent and a buyer's agent. However, you should not—and in some places, legally cannot—engage in a deal where the real estate agent represents both parties because there is a conflict of interest. Your agent should solely represent your best interests.

Lawyer

You might not see a lawyer in this process, but should you choose to undergo the purchase process without an agent, protect yourself from risk by involving a lawyer. People often opt for this route who have experience in purchasing property and want to find a better deal by cutting out intermediaries.

Architect

You may or may not have an architect. If you choose to have your tiny house designs custom-made, an architect will be responsible for those plans. The goal of the architect is to design a house for you that is safe and comfortable and conforms properly to its location. Like any other professional, ensure that the architect you work with has relevant experience and good references.

Insurance Providers

Insurance is a must for your tiny house, so you will likely work with an insurance agent or broker. An insurance agent works on behalf of an insurance company and represents their best interests, whereas an insurance broker is independent of the insurance company and represents you, working with several insurance companies to find you the best option. We will dive into insurance in Chapter 2, but know that you will certainly be working with someone in the insurance field.

ZONING BASICS

If you're reading this book, there is a good chance you're itching to resolve the zoning and code issue, which makes sense, given it is a massive barrier.

Zoning and code play similar yet distinct roles in the world of homeownership and construction. Zoning is the determination of how your land can be used and is determined by a local governing body, typically a county, city, or township. In some countries, like France and Germany, zoning is determined at a national level. Zoning is typically much more localized in countries where tiny houses are most popular, like the United States, Canada, and Australia. This correlation is no coincidence, but more on that in Chapter 3.

Zoning began as a response to runaway development in the early twentieth century. It is essentially a community's decision to make rules on how land can be used, so there is continuity in the look, feel, and property value of a given place. It ensures power plants don't get put up in the middle of a residential area or hotels next to a natural conservation area. In its ideal state, zoning serves this important purpose. In its more practical state, zoning rules make figuring out what you can and cannot do with land challenging and sometimes overly strict or unfair.

We will dive much deeper into zoning—and how to navigate it—later in the book. Until then, understand these basics when zoning is referenced.

CODE BASICS

Codes play a different role and are governed by local building departments, sometimes called planning departments. While zoning applies to land use, code applies to the design and construction of a house itself. The main code to consider is the building code, but there are other more specific codes like fire code and private sewage disposal code to consider as well.

Fundamentally, building codes are in place to keep people safe. Many of them are born out of past accidents. They exist to ensure that people building houses, be they contractors or DIY builders, are constructing them correctly. Like zoning, in the idealistic state, this sounds all well and good, but in the practical state, building codes can also seem daunting and overbearing. That doesn't negate the fact that building a safe home is incredibly important.

While governance of building code is localized, the building code itself is typically standardized. In the United States, building codes tend to adhere to 2018 International Residential Code (IRC) or 2021 IRC. There is even a recently added Appendix Q for tiny houses, which relaxes the code for houses under 400 square feet on a fixed foundation.

More to come on code, but now you at least have a sense of what it is.

MISCONCEPTIONS & NON-EXISTENT LOOPHOLES

Let's debunk some myths.

The main reason we need to do this is that if you don't, you may be operating under false assumptions that can come back to hurt you. This can result in having to pay money you're not expecting or simply don't have, having to move your tiny house against your will, or simply finding out one day that you did things incorrectly and are at risk.

In no particular order, here are some tiny house misconceptions and loopholes that don't exist:

- **"Building a tiny house on a trailer makes it an RV"**…while this *can* be true, it is not automatically true. In the United States, a tiny house on wheels is considered an RV only if it is certified by the RV Industry Association, also known as RVIA. To obtain an RVIA certification, you must have your tiny house on wheels built by an RVIA-certified builder and have proof of the certification in hand, typically in the form of a seal. This misconception matters because if you find zoning laws that allow RVs in certain places and think that your uncertified tiny house is an RV, you are actually breaking the zoning ordinance.

- **"You don't need a building permit because the house is below minimum square footage"**...this is a foolish way to skirt the process of getting permits. The reality is that if you are building a home, you are supposed to get building permits. Think about this from the perspective of the building department. If they were to see your project in motion, and you were to tell them, "this house is too small; I don't need permits," do you think that the inspector is going to allow it? Probably not.

- **"Just say that your tiny house is an RV, camper, or vehicle"**...similar to the previous non-loophole, this approach relies on using a technicality to hoodwink inspectors. Again, it won't work. If it is not certified as an RV, it isn't an RV. If it looks like a house, they will treat it as such unless you have proof or prior agreement otherwise. This is one more reason you should work with—not against—your local councils.

- **"Deny that your structure is permanent"**...this one might actually work, but it is risky. It is more likely to work if the inspector or the local zoning board is on-board with the interpretation of the ordinance. The issue with this approach is that if you rely on it as a response to questioning, you will be in the hands of the inspector. Plus, if you say that the house is movable, and you are living in a space zoned for short-term residence, then be prepared to prove it…by moving.

- **"If the tiny house has a license plate, it falls under DMV jurisdiction"**…this is another flavor of some of the other technicality-based arguments for skirting regulation. Frankly, it is like trying to speak legalities with a lawyer, you are going to get tied up in knots and lose the argument quickly. Unless you genuinely understand how the jurisdictions work and are ready to fight an expert on this, don't take this approach.

- **"You will probably be fine"**…while this may be true in many cases, it is not recommended if you can avoid it. Generally speaking, many people choose to live in a tiny house under-the-radar or simply have no other option. Many simply cannot afford to go through the process of acquiring permits, hiring architects, or finding new land. Many others may have the funds needed but cannot navigate their area's zoning and code hurdles. There is merit to this lax approach, but it is not without risk, and those risks must be known if you choose this route. You will need to ask yourself: *Can I afford to pay fines? What happens if someone gets hurt in my house that is not up to code? What will I do if a zoning board asks me to leave my land?* Ultimately, you may read this book and still choose this route, and that is ok; just know the risks.

Ultimately, tiny house codes and zoning are hard to navigate. That is why there is so much misinformation about ways to get around it. But you have to remember that ignoring the rules does not exempt you from those rules.

Remember that plenty of people are living in tiny houses completely lawfully, and the number is only growing as more areas adopt pro-tiny-house regulations and standards. Zoning and building departments want to work with you and will work with you. Don't see them as something to avoid and evade. You can legally live in a tiny house if you decide it is important!

THE TINY HOUSE MINDSET

We haven't even gotten into the meat of the content, but we have already covered a lot.

You might be feeling a bit overwhelmed or feel like giving up, but I urge you to reconsider.

Think of this process as a learning experience and an adventure. You will encounter roadblocks and frustration, you will deal with helpful people and others who are not, and you will need to be patient. But you will also create something incredible that can improve your life. A little bit of short-term sacrifice is worth it.

To make sure that this adventure is a fruitful one, there are a few key principles to follow.

The first is to reduce risk. That means reducing the risk of overspending and reducing the risk that your tiny house is not within regulation. You should never embark on a large project without a clear understanding of the financials and the ways disaster can strike.

Second, have a support system. Going about this life change on your own can be difficult and scary. Build a team to at least support you through the change, if not actively help on the project. The process will be much more enjoyable this way. Many tiny house owners say that one of the most powerful elements of the tiny house transition is the strengthening of existing relationships and the creation of new ones.

Third, be positive and patient. Specifically, be positive and patient with the people that are helping you. That means being respectful and pleasant with sellers, zoning departments, lenders, contractors, laborers, real estate agents, and anyone else involved in your process. As they say, you catch more flies with honey than with vinegar.

Fourth, and at the risk of being corny, persevere. You are going to run into issues that you need to solve. It doesn't matter your experience, intelligence, or wealth; if you are determined to live the tiny house life, you can and you will. Don't give up.

TINY HOUSE FINANCIALS

Most people begin their tiny house land search with one single number in mind. They say, "my budget is X amount of money," and then they start looking for land, tiny houses, or both.

Having this single amount in mind is important, but it is just the beginning. You must understand *how* you will spend that money. Like building a tiny house with no blueprints, ignoring the financials means you are going into this project without a clear plan. If you choose to pursue a tiny house without a rock-solid financial plan, the risk of outspending your budget or draining your bank account before your project ends is significantly higher.

Because affordability is the basis for all other decisions, we will cover it before we even talk about land. You must understand the details of your budget now and in the future, how to manage risk, what hidden costs are involved, and your options for financing and insurance.

KNOW YOUR PROJECT BUDGET & EXPECTED EXPENSES

Most people have a basic sense of what they can afford, but a single dollar amount is not enough. You must know what the expenses will *actually* be. Here is a comprehensive list of the expenses and the amount of money you can expect to spend in general.

The Land - $10,000+

The land is typically one of the most expensive components of owning a tiny house, along with setting up the land itself. If you already own the land or plan to use a tiny house community, this doesn't apply. If you go the tiny house community route, still expect to pay in the form of community fees or lot fees.

For purchasing land, you can spend millions of dollars on large parcels or a few thousand on small parcels. The more developed the land is, the more expensive it will be per acre/square kilometer. The more raw the land is, the cheaper it will be per acre/square kilometer, but it will not necessarily be cheap to make livable, as you may need to connect the land to the grid or make other changes.

Land loans are an option but are not the same as a mortgage. Expect to spend between 30% and 60% down on a land loan. The more improved the land is, the likelier you are to qualify for a lower down payment and lower interest rate. We will cover financing in detail later in this chapter.

Setting Up The Land - $20,000+

This cost is so variable it is impossible to assign a single cost, but first-time land buyers easily overlook it. In the land developer world, it is common to budget more for the setup of land than the actual purchase of the land!

Land has three distinctions:

- **Raw land**: This is land that is completely undeveloped, with no roads, electricity, or sewers. It is the cheapest to buy and the hardest to finance. Many going fully off-grid seek this option.
- **Unimproved land**: This land has some utilities set up but is not yet ready for a new home. It may have electricity to the property but no

electrical meter or gas meter. It is more expensive than raw land but easier to finance.

- **Improved land**: Improved land is more or less ready for home construction. It is the most expensive but the easiest to finance of the three land options.

Generally speaking, the setup cost averages around $20,000, but it changes depending on what you need to do or don't do. If you are buying a parcel of land that does not have utilities set up and intend to live on-grid, then you can expect to pay quite a bit for the land after purchase.

The biggest variables are the cost to connect to electricity, municipal water, and municipal sewer. In some cases, you may be close enough to the public system that it is free. In other cases, you may be so far away that it costs tens of thousands of dollars. Think in the realm of $10,000 per quarter mile (400 meters). To accurately estimate this amount, you will need to get an estimate from the local planning department or a local services company.

That said, it is certainly easier to opt for improved land if you can find and afford it. If raw or unimproved land is the route you must take, make sure you budget appropriately for additional expenses, research what it will cost to set up, and be prepared to explain your plans in-depth with lenders and zoning and building departments.

Some other land setup costs to consider:

- **Driveway:** Depending on the type of driveway, expect to spend by the square foot or square meter. Gravel runs between $1.25 and $1.80 per square foot (930 square centimeters). Concrete is in the $4-$15 per square foot range, and asphalt will cost you $7-$15 per square foot. If you opt to install your own gravel driveway, DIY materials are about $1 per square foot.

- **Impact Fees and In Lieu Fees:** Some cities, towns, and states require that developers pay an impact fee, which is designed to offset the cost of public services that new development requires. In Lieu fees are similar to impact fees but are meant to offset the environmental impact. You may need to pay both, one, or neither of these, and the fees vary from pennies per square foot to set fees in the five-figure range. Your local building department can inform you of these and any other fees you will need to pay before receiving your building permits.

- **Land surveying:** If your local zoning department or courthouse doesn't already have records of the latest land survey, you may be required to get the land surveyed to acquire zoning permits. Surveying the land is the process of having a professional surveyor determine exactly where the boundaries of the land exist. In most cases, this costs around $500, but it can be much more expensive in certain jurisdictions and circumstances. Discuss with the zoning department whether surveying is necessary, and if it is, what kind of survey is required.

- **Septic System:** If you do not connect to municipal sewage and don't plan to rely on an off-grid blackwater and greywater system, septic is a go-to alternative. Sophisticated systems will run you upwards of $20,000, while a basic tank should only cost you $3,000.

- **Well Installation:** If you do not connect to municipal water, and don't plan to source your water purely from rainwater collection, then a well is a great option. The cost to drill a well is linearly related to the depth of the well, typically ranging from $15-$25 per foot (30 centimeters) just to drill and ranging from $25-$61 per foot to completely install. The average final cost of a well will range between $3,750 and $15,300.

- **Water treatment:** You may need to treat the water that you source from a well or choose to treat the water that you source from public water. For full-home systems, expect to pay between $900 and $3,000.
- **Land Clearing & Preparation:** If you buy woodland property, you may need to remove some trees and prepare the land for construction. Small-scale projects average less than $1,000, while larger properties in heavily-wooded areas average around $8,000. While clearing the land is reasonable from an expense perspective, preparing the land for construction is significantly more expensive. This potential cost may be another reason to consider the tiny house on wheels, as it only requires a level surface but not prepared land for laying a foundation. Preparing 1,000 square feet (93 square meters) averages $1,200 to $2,000.
- **Land grading and drainage:** It is unpleasant and potentially unsafe for water to sit idly around your home, as it can cause structural rot and mold. Grading, which is the reforming of the land, and drainage, which is the redirection of water, are two options you may need to

consider to move water away from your home properly. There are various options, including French drains, flow wells, and dry creek beds. Regardless of the project, understand that this may be needed. The cost here will vary significantly based on how much the land needs to be modified, where you live, and what type and size drain you will need. Based on US national averages, drainage systems cost between $2,000 and $6,000 to have installed, while grading costs $3,100 on average.

- **Soil Testing:** As we will unpack later, when buying land with no municipal sewage and the intention to install septic, you must pass a soil test–also known as a perc test–to purchase the land. In some cases, you may be required by the building department to pass a perc test even if you plan to live off-grid without a septic system, as it could be a requirement for building permits. The soil tests range from $750 to $1,850 on average.

It may feel daunting seeing about ten expense items in addition to setting up electricity, water, and sewage. Certainly, this list is extensive, but remember that very few people need to take care of every single item on this list. Nevertheless, it is important to account for all these possibilities in the budget, and know to look for these hidden costs before you buy a property.

Building a Tiny House - $25,000-$60,000

While there is no doubt that you *could* build a tiny house for less than $10,000, the reality is that this takes a substantial amount of creativity and patience, as it requires a lot of repurposed materials. If you are going to build using new materials, expect a minimum of $25,000 in expenses, including the hired labor to assist in the build.

This cost has proven to be quite variable because it depends on the cost of lumber and the material supply chain. When the COVID–19 pandemic hit, material costs skyrocketed. While the pandemic may have been a phenomenon, the variability of construction costs is not.

It is worth adding that you can receive a personal or construction loan from the bank, which will typically require that you put down 20-30%. Note that construction loans are typically short-term, lasting only 12 to 18 months.

Additionally, if you are building your own tiny house, you may want to become a certified builder by the RVIA or NOAH, the organizations that control RV certification and mobile home certification, respectively. At the time of publishing, DIY builders could become NOAH certified for a DIY build for $504. Becoming an RVIA builder is much more difficult, involved, and expensive. Plus, it is not intended for DIY builders but actual manufacturers. For those living outside the United States, research RV and mobile home certification in your country to understand how to navigate this component of building to standards.

Buying a Tiny House - $25,000-$250,000

Buying a prebuilt tiny house costs a lot. A lot of estimates are outdated and low. Don't expect to spend less than $60,000 for a new tiny house. Don't expect to spend less than $25,000 for a decent yet low-end used one. If you want some luxury or need space for multiple people, the cost will increase quickly. It is not unheard of to spend well over $200,000 for a tiny house these days.

While you probably won't be able to get a mortgage for a tiny house, you may use a personal loan or seller financing. If you opt for this route, expect to put 20-30% down.

Permits - $400-$2,000

You likely need to acquire building permits from your local building department, and failing to do so is at your own peril. These are essentially city, county, or municipality authorizations to build your home. Permit costs can vary greatly; in some rural areas incentivizing development, you may only pay $100, but in major cities, you can easily see permits in the several thousand dollar range. Expect somewhere in the middle, between $400 and $2,000. The average is $1,200 in the United States. Other countries also have building permits, typically in a similar price range.

Professional Services - $0-$20,000

You may need to hire some professionals, or several professionals, to help you with your process. Ideally, you only need a real estate agent that is paid a commission by the seller of the land or home. In this scenario, you won't spend any money on professional services.

However, there are some situations where you will pay for a professional:

- **Real estate agent**: While the seller typically pays the commission, there is a chance that you will have to pay your agent's commission. In this case, expect to spend 5-10% of the closing price of the land or home that you buy. Just check with your agent before buying the land. This structure is not that common, but it does exist.

- **Lawyer**: If you are navigating a particularly difficult or extraordinary situation, you may find hiring a lawyer beneficial. If you don't have a buyer's agent, you will need a lawyer to draft the contract. Real estate lawyers average around $250 per hour.

- **Architect**: For those going the route of a custom house plan, expect to pay an architect a substantial amount. Architects often charge around 5-20% of the overall project cost, so a $50,000 tiny house build will be at least $2,500. Some architects charge hourly instead, between $125 and $250 per hour. A small handful of architects charge by the square foot, anywhere from $2 to $10 per, though this approach is less common. Based on all the above, expect to spend anywhere from $2,000 to $20,000 or more for plans. This reality is why many aspiring tiny house owners opt for stock plans and kits.

Downsizing & Moving - $0 - $1,000

The process of moving can be an opportunity to sell many of your belongings and make some money, but even still, you will likely spend more than you earn. If your tiny house is near your current home, you may be able to transition for a negligible amount of money.

However, if you are moving far away and don't have a lot of help, you may need to hire a moving company. Be sure to factor this expense into the equation.

Sample Cost Breakdown

Given all of the information on cost above, let's do a *sample* breakdown of expenses.

In this hypothetical, let's imagine the following:

- Janet has decided to build her own tiny house on wheels using reputable design plans that she found online for **$1,000**. Her estimated expense for the build is $33,000, but she has allocated **$40,000** to account for unforeseen costs in the construction process. She will pay for this in cash.
- Janet has found a perfect 4-acre (16,000 square meters) plot of raw land with a little creek running through the woods in the back. The seller is asking for $23,000, but Janet's real estate agent thinks she can get the price down to **$21,000**. She will pay for this in cash.
- The land is not hooked up to any utility systems. Janet will hook up to the electrical grid, since the electrical lines are relatively close to the property. The planning department has quoted her **$2,500**. However, she does not have

access to municipal water or sewage. Instead, she will have to drill a well and install a septic system, which will cost about **$10,000** and **$7,500**, respectively, based on a quote from a local drilling company. She has determined that she won't need to remove any trees, but she will need to lay a 40-foot gravel driveway, which she will do herself. At about $1 per square foot, she anticipates spending **$400** on the driveway. She will also need to install a French drain, which has been quoted to **$2,000** by a local contractor. Her land will not need any grading, nor will she need to lay a foundation or prepare the land for one since she will have a tiny house on wheels.

- The property has not had a soil test, so Janet will need to pay for one of those upfront to install a septic system. That will cost **$1,000**. There are no impact fees, but she does need to get the land surveyed since there are no recent records. This survey will cost **$500**. Additionally, the building department has informed her that the building permits will cost **$1,300**.

- Janet has a real estate agent representing her, but the seller will pay the agent's commission.

Janet does not have a lawyer, nor did she use an architect.

- Janet anticipates spending **$500** to cover the movers.

Using the above example, let's break down what Janet's costs will be:

Janet's Example Item	Janet's Example Cost
Tiny House Build	$40,000
Land	$21,000
Well Installation	$10,000
Septic System	$7,500
Electrical Hookup	$2,500
Drain Installation	$2,000
Building Permits	$1,300
Soil/Perc Test	$1,000
Design Plans	$1,000
Survey	$500
Move-in	$500
Driveway	$400
TOTAL	**$87,700**

While the above scenario is just an example, it uses the realistic ranges discussed throughout this chapter. Your project will certainly differ from Janet's, and you shouldn't skip the process of budgeting for yourself. The takeaway of this sample budget is to show you that your tiny house and land purchase must be only a portion of the budget. In the example above, the tiny house and land account for $61,000, but the overall project is $87,700. That means that 30% of the project cost is *not* the cost of the build and the land.

While this can undoubtedly appear overwhelming, it is vital to understand these expenses going in. If you have a budget of only $40,000, you cannot use it all on the house and the land even if you plan to go off-grid and ignore the local regulations.

For this reason, it is imperative that you meticulously calculate the expenses from the point of starting the search for land to the point of moving into your tiny house. The last thing you want is to be out tens of thousands with an incomplete project and no money left.

FINANCING

As mentioned above and throughout this chapter, financing is an option. When you consider your budget, you should not just consider the budget that you have available in cash but also how you can use a lender to your advantage.

You will rarely get a mortgage for a tiny house unless it is a traditional home that just so happens to be less than 400 square feet. However, there are many types of loans available. As tiny house prices increase, this option is becoming more and more common.

Before even asking what type of loan, first understand who is providing the loan. If you have a relationship with an existing bank, speak to them. Regardless, you will likely have more luck with small community banks and credit unions. They are often less rigid and more eager to earn your business. Don't be too discouraged if you get rejected. You may have to talk to several institutions before finding a lender that approves you.

For buying the tiny house itself, you have three options:

- **Seller Financing**: While you could potentially find an owner of a current tiny house willing to finance the sale, the chances are slim. Typically, seller financing is an option when you go through a company that builds tiny houses. They may finance it themselves or partner with a specific lender on your behalf. The payment schedule and down payment on seller financing vary.

- **Personal Loan:** The personal loan is a simple kind of loan. You request up to $100,000 in cash from a lender and pay it back with interest over time. Interest typically comes in around 9% but can be as low as 3% or as high as 36%, depending on your credit. This option works particularly well if you have good credit (610 or higher) or a strong relationship with a bank or credit union. That said, personal loans often don't require collateral. Personal loans typically range from 12 months to 48 months, occasionally up to 7 years.

- **Home Equity Loan:** For those that already own a house and are buying a tiny house as a second home or ADU, the home equity loan is a special type of loan that uses your primary residence as collateral, offsetting or removing the need for cash. These loans typically range from 5 to 30 years, require a minimum credit score of 620, and carry an interest rate of 3% to 11%.

For financing the land and construction, there are a handful of options as well:

- **New Construction Loan:** A new construction loan, also known as a lot loan, typically covers not just the labor and materials but also the land, closing costs, plans, permits, fees, contingency reserves in case the project costs more than expected, and interest reserves in case you don't want to make interest payments during the build. All of this bundled up makes new construction loans enticing and quite valuable. However, most lenders typically require 20-30% down, expect a credit score above 680, may use the finished home as collateral for remaining payments, and will rigorously inspect your building plans and builder. Plus, the loan typically only lasts 12-18 months and carries a variable rate that is typically 1% higher than the set mortgage rate. If you are building it yourself, this loan may be out of the question. DIY builders will require the owner-builder type of construction loan, where you act as the general contractor for your construction project. This loan type is risky to the bank and, therefore, difficult to attain. It is typically only granted to those who are professional contractors. If you go this route, it is recommended that you get prequalified well in advance of the project, considering new construction loans are harder to acquire than mortgages. Construction loans come in three forms. One is the construction-only loan, which only covers the construction and then must be paid off or refinanced. One is the construction-to-permanent loan, which finances the construction and the finished home, making the finished home collateral. The third is the owner-builder loan previously mentioned.

- **Land Loan:** For the purchase of the land only, you can acquire a land loan. While this typically requires a high credit score of 720 or better, the land loan is less rigorous than the new construction loan and better suited for people who don't need to finance a build. The rawer the land, the harder it will be to get approved and the higher the interest rates will be, but that tends to be offset by the lower cost of purchasing raw land. The opposite is true with improved land. Land loans don't typically require collateral, but they require 30-60% down, have a duration of 2 to 7 years, and have interest rates of a minimum of 4% but often much higher. It varies significantly.

- **Personal Loan:** Just as with purchasing the house, a personal loan is an option for purchasing land.

- **Seller Financing:** Seller financing is an option with land, where the land owner acts as the lender. The issue with this approach is that there is somewhat of a legal gray area as to who actually owns the land. The seller retains the legal title of the property until you pay it off, which takes some of the control out of your hands. If you and the seller do opt for seller financing, it is wise to bring a lawyer in to help you with the terms and conditions. Rates and down payments vary.

- **SBA 504 Loan:** This loan is an option for those based in the United States that are planning to start a tiny house business, such as a tiny house community. While the rates of the loan are dependent upon the length and current market rates, the SBA 504 loan has a significant upside: it reduces your down payment to 10%. The SBA picks up 40%, and the lender picks up 50% of the loan. These loans come in 10 and 20-year durations. Since the SBA loan is competitive, you stand a better chance with a credit score of at least 680, preferably 720.

- **USDA Rural Housing Loan:** Another US-based option, this loan is designed for low-to-middle-income families looking for a primary residence in qualified rural areas, typically those with populations under 20,000 people. This population size makes up a surprisingly large portion of the country. Section 523 loans allow buyers to build their own homes, while Section 524 allows buyers to hire contractors. The rates are fixed but typically quite low depending on your credit score, and there is no down payment needed, which is a huge advantage for those lacking cash. Most lenders require a minimum credit score of 640, and the loan duration varies from 2 years to 30 or more years.

Type of Loan	Part of Project	Typical Minimum Credit	Typical Down Payment, Collateral, Requirements	Typical Interest Rate	Typical Length
Seller Financing	Land, Tiny House	Varies	Varies	Varies	Varies
Personal Loan	Land, Tiny House, Construction	610	$0	3-36%	1-4 years
Home Equity Loan	Tiny House	620	Primary residence as collateral	3-11%	5-30 years
New Construction Loan (not DIY)	Everything	680	20-30% down, possibly uses finished construction as collateral	~1% higher than mortgage rate	12-18 months
New Construction Loan (DIY)	Everything	680	20-30% down, possible uses finished construction as collateral, requires DIY builder is a professional	~1% higher than mortgage rate	12-18 months
Land Loan	Land	720	30-60% down	4-35%	2-7 years
SBA 504	Everything (if starting a business)	690	10% down	Based on market	10 year, 20 year
	Everything (if in a qualified rural area)	640	0% down	Low, based on market	2-30 years

When it comes to financing, it is best to explore your various options, check current market rates, and seek help when you need it. Financing is often the missing piece that will enable you to turn your unaffordable tiny house project into an affordable one. Consider getting a financial planner involved.

ALTERNATIVE OPTIONS TO OWNING LAND OR A TINY HOUSE

Homeownership is often synonymous with tiny house life. People want to live freely without ongoing expenses and want a home they can call their own.

With that said, you can choose to forgo owning land, a tiny house, or both. There is no shame in doing so.

Renting

For many people, renting is a great way to save money over time, so they can make a purchase later, especially since living tiny should save you money in the long run!

Renting also has other advantages, especially if you live in a tiny house on wheels. For one, you can lease land and live on it as you need, then leave relatively easily if you need to or decide to. Ultimately, renting equates to flexibility. For younger tiny house owners or those who are nomadic in general, this provides substantial freedom. Some may also consider this a wise choice when just beginning your tiny house journey.

Plenty of websites exist for tiny house owners to connect with landowners, including Facebook Marketplace, Hipcamp, Land Lease Exchange, and Landlease.-com. Do a little bit of digging. Consider a tiny house community as well. Many of them have tiny houses for rent.

Subsistence & Exchange

There are options for an alternative arrangement with a farm or ranch, where you live in a tiny house on the property where you work. It is common for housing to be provided at larger operations, but for smaller farms, you may not have any accommodation. Instead, the farm owner may allow you to live on their land in your tiny house, eliminating any need to purchase or rent land. Some popular platforms to find an exchange like this include Workaway, Worldpackers, and WWOOF.

Buy or Rent an RV

A lot of people roll their eyes when RVs are mentioned, but they provide a valuable alternative to at least consider.

On the plus side, they are pre-built, mobile, and clearly defined in the eyes of the law. Their downside is the stigma and visual appeal (though many are pretty nice these days), the lack of customizability, and the lack of vertical space compared to a tiny house.

Nevertheless, don't rule the RV out if you are seeking a tiny house purely for financial freedom or mobility but could care less about how it looks.

UNDERSTAND THE ONGOING BUDGET

The tiny house cost upfront is significant, but the ongoing budget is equally—if not more— important in your decision to go tiny. Make sure you do the math. Before and during the process, you should always answer and reanswer the following two questions:

1. *How much do I currently spend each month?*
2. *How much will I spend each month once I live in my tiny house?*

For many whose goal is financial freedom, the answer to the second question must be less than the answer to the first question for this whole tiny house endeavor to be worthwhile.

For those going tiny as a second home or for non-financial reasons, answer these questions to confirm that you can afford to pursue the tiny house life.

Aside from typical living expenses that everyone faces, here are the ongoing expenses that you need to consider for a tiny house:

- **Ongoing payments as a result of financing:** In the event that you do finance your tiny house or the land it is on, your new monthly expense will include these monthly payments for the duration of the loan.
- **Gasoline**: For owners of mobile tiny houses, you will have to pay for the cost to tow these homes, which will considerably increase your gasoline expense. Account for the variability in gasoline costs.
- **Commuting:** For owners of tiny houses that remain in one place, understand if your commute changes. If it does, account for the added cost of your new commute.
- **Groceries and household items:** Since tiny houses don't have room for much stuff, you will probably not be buying groceries and household items in bulk, as you simply won't have room. That means groceries will be marginally more expensive in a tiny house. Look at your latest receipts and identify which items you buy in bulk. The next time you go shopping, observe the difference in the unit

cost between bulk and non-bulk items and multiply that difference by the number of non-bulk items required to make up a bulk purchase. You now know what a trip to the grocery store will cost when you live in a tiny house.

- **Storage**: While certainly avoidable, you may keep some of your items but not have them in a tiny house. If that is the case, make sure you account for the cost of a storage unit.

- **Insurance**: You absolutely need tiny house insurance. This protects the home from damage and protects you from liability. Opting out of insurance is one of the biggest mistakes you can make. More to come on this topic.

- **Utilities**: Whether you are going the off-grid route or the traditional on-grid route, your utilities should decrease in cost. At a minimum, you have less electrical usage. However, if you are not connected to municipal water, you will learn to reduce water usage as well by necessity, which means lower water bills.

- **Maintenance**: For existing homeowners, this is already built into your budget, but for first-time homeowners, you always must account for maintenance and repair as an ongoing expense. A general rule is to budget 1-4% of your home value for annual maintenance. For example, if you have a $60,000 tiny house, budget $600-$2,400 per year, which is $50-$200 per month. It is recommended that you lean on the side of more maintenance to be safe. At least account for some maintenance and repair.

- **Tax**: If this is your first time owning property, know there will be a property tax. Property tax varies depending on where you live, but listings typically include the annual tax. Look up property tax for your area, so you know what to expect.

- **HOA Fee**: If you choose to live in a development or a tiny house community, expect to pay Homeowners Association Fees. These typically vary from $100 per month for less involved developments to $700 per month for much more luxurious and all-inclusive areas.

As you think long-term about the cost of the tiny house, you may also find yourself wondering whether or not you can make money off of your tiny house. While there is no doubt that people are building and selling new tiny houses for a profit, used tiny houses depreciate, similar to how a car depreciates. You are unlikely to sell your tiny house for a profit. The exception to this general rule is if your tiny house is on a foundation and tied to the land it is on, in which case you can build equity in the house. The recent supply chain shortage of the pandemic has also made reselling tiny houses more popular, so there is a current trend. It is difficult to say where that trend will lead.

With all that said, you should not enter into the tiny house life with the thought that it will make you money in the long run as an investment vehicle. Instead, you should consider your tiny house as an investment that *saves* you money over time. The exception to this rule is using a tiny house as a rental property, which is an in-depth topic not in the scope of this book.

INSURANCE

Tiny house insurance is non-negotiable. While you may not be required to get it, you are crazy not to.

Tiny houses deal with typical tiny house issues like fire and water damage or destruction. Tiny houses also get stolen and vandalized and can be destroyed in a highway accident. What happens if you don't have insurance? In short, nothing.

Plus, if you go through a lender or plan to take your tiny house on the road, you likely *will* be required to insure your tiny house.

Here are your options:

RV Insurance

The RV insurance option only works if your tiny house is certifiably an RV. In the United States, that means having a Recreational Vehicle Industry Association (RVIA) certification. To attain this certification, an RVIA-certified builder must build your tiny house on wheels.

Generally speaking, RV insurance is best suited for those that tend to move their tiny house frequently, every few months or so. In other words, if you use your tiny house like you would use an RV, this insurance is a good way to go.

If you qualify for it, RV insurance is quite valuable. You will want to get the policy designed for full-time residents if you are planning to live in the tiny house full-time.

Here is what you can expect from an RV policy from a coverage perspective, but of course, read the fine print of your actual policy as this list is generic in nature:

- **Collision:** Coverage in the event your tiny house is damaged in an accident.

- **Comprehensive**: Coverage in the event of theft, vandalism, fire, weather-related incidents, falling objects, etc.
- **Liability**: Coverage for property damages and injuries caused by you.
- **Uninsured/Underinsured Motorist:** Coverage in the event you are in an accident with someone that doesn't have enough insurance. It should cover damages to the tiny house, as well as personal injury and lost wages, if applicable.
- **Personal Property:** Coverage of your belongings within the tiny house in the event they are damaged, destroyed, or lost.
- **Medical:** Coverage for medical bills of you and your passengers if your tiny house has an accident.

Mobile Home Insurance

The mobile home policy, or manufactured home policy, is better suited to the less nomadic tiny house owner. If you only move your tiny house once or twice a year, or less, mobile home insurance is probably a more economical choice. Like the RV, you cannot simply declare your tiny house a mobile home; it has to be certified, at least in most developed countries. In the United States, that means getting a tiny house built to NOAH standards by a NOAH-certified builder. You can become a NOAH-certified builder for your DIY project before starting, which can help gain the vote of confidence that the organization provides, helping insurers classify your tiny house as a mobile home.

Mobile home insurance is similar to standard home-owners insurance. Be sure to understand your coverage in detail, as you may require additional coverage depending on your situation. Here is what you can expect in general:

- **Personal Property:** Coverage for your belongings within the tiny house in the event they are damaged, destroyed, or lost.
- **Physical Damage:** Coverage for accidental damage to the interior or exterior of the home or other structures on the property. Physical damage typically does not include flood, earthquake, or wildfire coverage, so look into this coverage separately. These policies also don't typically cover damage due to lack of maintenance.
- **Liability**: Coverage for property damages and injuries caused by you.

Named Peril Insurance Policies & All Risks Policies

This policy can be enticing as primary insurance because it is often inexpensive. Still, many in the insurance industry recommend using this type of policy only for additional coverage to your primary insurance for outstanding risks, such as earthquakes or flooding. A peril policy covers losses incurred from events or hazards named on the policy, and that is it. The burden of proof is on the uninsured, so you will be required to prove the peril that caused the damage.

All risks policies are the opposite of a peril policy. They cover all perils *except* for those named in the policy.

Tiny Home Specialist Insurance Providers

If navigating your tiny house insurance coverage is confusing, too much work, or simply not bearing fruit, you can contact a tiny home insurance specialist. There are an increasing number of them as tiny houses become more popular.

Since these companies are specific to tiny houses, they have experience with the insurance of tiny homes, as well as alternative living structures like ADUs, container homes, off-grid cabins, and more. They will offer a lot of flexibility and options to ensure you are covered. Best of all, they will usually cover houses not certified by RVIA or NOAH.

Other Insurance Considerations

There are some circumstances where you need to look for other insurance coverage. For example, if you plan to rent out your tiny house on a platform like Airbnb or Vrbo, you will likely need short-term renters insurance. If you plan to rent it out long-term, you should check out landlord insurance. For anyone creating a tiny house community or embarking on an entrepreneurial tiny house venture, talk to an independent insurance broker to figure out what coverage you need.

Cost and Providers:

Now that you understand the various types of insurance, you may still be wondering where to actually get the insurance.

You can start by searching online for tiny house insurance providers, and checking out various financially-focused websites that review insurance providers for tiny houses. Another good approach is to contact anyone within your network who owns a home or a business, as they may have a relationship with an insurance broker. The benefit of an insurance broker is that they are a third-party seller that represents the buyer, whereas an insurance agent represents the insurance company. A broker can contact various insurance companies on your behalf to help you find the right policy.

As far as costs, your insurance will vary depending on your policy. Your house's location, whether or not it is stationary, who built it, whether or not it is certified, and how it is used all play a role in determining your policy and its cost.

To give a rough estimate, expect tiny house insurance to range from $400 to $1,500 annually.

THE RIGHT FINANCIAL MINDSET

Many people joining the tiny house movement are underprepared for the financial intricacies of becoming a tiny house owner. While there is undoubtedly more to it than just knowing your budget, the financial element of this project is not super complex. It boils down to asking yourself a few key questions we have addressed throughout the chapter:

1. What is my overall budget?
2. How much will it cost upfront to acquire the land and buy or build the house?
3. What are my other costs to consider before I move into a tiny house, such as preparing the land?

4. Should I finance any portion of my project, and if so, how?
5. What costs will I have ongoing, including living expenses and insurance?

Answer these questions as best you can now. As you embark on the journey towards tiny life, keep revisiting the questions and adjusting your answers. These are moving targets but pivotal all the same. Embrace them, and you will ensure that this transition to a tiny house is a financial success.

ANALYZING LAND & NAVIGATING ZONING

L and is the single biggest hurdle for those seeking to live in a tiny house. Regardless of country, state, city, or province, people have a hard time finding land that is not only affordable but also zoned properly. In a recent study, 35% of respondents listed land-related issues as a main barrier to becoming tiny house owners. Luckily, with some diligence and focus, you can overcome this barrier.

In this chapter, we will first walk through how to think about land and the land-buying process, covering the step-by-step tasks you can expect. We will then discuss the types of land to consider and ways to find land for sale and rent. Finally, we will dive deep into zoning and how to navigate it.

THE IMPORTANCE OF FLEXIBILITY

I have had many conversations with aspiring tiny house owners with rigid limitations on where they will live. Sometimes, someone will tell me something like this: "I want to live in a tiny house on private land in the state of Virginia within an hour from Washington, D.C."

Without a doubt, there are good reasons for this desire. Perhaps a commute to work requires that you live close to a specific major city, or maybe your grandchildren live in the area, or maybe you have always lived there and don't want to leave home. These reasons are all valid, and you should consider them.

You also need to realize that finding land for a tiny house requires flexibility. Most major metropolitan areas prohibit tiny houses, aside from secondary homes on property with an existing primary residence, which are called ADUs. There are some exceptions in some cities that are tiny house-friendly, such as Portland, Oregon, but generally speaking, tiny houses are found in rural areas. In fact, an estimated 70% of tiny houses are rural, largely because land is cheaper and better zoned for tiny house life. While this reality is improving in many places, it is still quite challenging.

This dilemma comes back to one of the main questions you should be asking yourself: *why do I want to live in a tiny house?* If you have a crystal clear vision of what a tiny house provides you, you can weigh those benefits against the sacrifices you must make.

In answering this question, you also will be able to identify what areas will work for you. Maybe you are willing to move across the country. Maybe you are only open to a 50 mile radius of your current home. On the flip side, challenge your own beliefs. For example, you may have it ingrained that you have to live in Montana because you have always wanted to live in Montana, but when you ask yourself *why* you want to live in Montana, you may realize that, in reality, you just want to live in a place in the Northern Rocky Mountains where you can mountain bike in the summer and ski in the winter. This realization now opens up Idaho, Wyoming, and Canada as possible locations for your tiny house.

Regardless, fit the place to the specific tiny house life you desire, not the other way around. The tiny house is the tool, not the goal!

THE PROCESS OF FINDING LAND FOR SALE

The land buying process requires patience and diligence. A lot of steps happen before you get into purchasing the land itself. In fact, this whole chapter covers the process of finding land while the next chapter covers buying land. Our goal here is simply to identify land that *could* have a tiny house on it.

You might wonder: *why is it so difficult?* The truth is that finding land is dependent on zoning, and zoning is dependent on location. Within the United States alone, there are more than 3,000 counties and municipalities, each with its own zoning rules. Canada, the United Kingdom, Australia, and New Zealand are similarly decentralized. Some exceptions exist, like in Germany and France, where zoning is centralized and controlled nationally. Still, for most tiny house owners, localized zoning is the main reason land search is so messy. Nevertheless, we must figure it out!

Several steps will happen. Their order may deviate slightly, and you may need to revisit some steps, but generally, here is what you can expect:

1. Identify the general area where you want to live.
2. Get in touch with a real estate agent. Remember that they are only paid once the sale is made and typically by the seller, so you have nothing to lose by working with an agent, as long as you remember that they are incentivized for you to buy. You may want to

do this after you have gone through steps 3 through 8 a couple of times, just so that you can have better ownership of the process in general.

3. Identify the parcels that interest you.

4. Identify the county, city, or town in which those parcels are located.

5. Find the county, city, or town zoning department website.

6. Find the GIS or parcel view map, as well as the zoning ordinance table, to identify zoning for the parcels you are seeking. If the zoning does not suit your needs, go back to the beginning. If the zoning does suit your needs, move on to the next step.

7. Write down any questions you have for the zoning department. Pick up the phone and call them. Be open about your plan for a tiny house and listen to their advice. If they tell you to do any follow-up steps, complete those steps.

8. Get written confirmation that the zoning department is okay with your plan. This email exchange is not a formal approval but more of an agreement that you can use the land as you see fit and that the zoning department will work with you when you own the land and need zoning board approval.

9. Do your due diligence on expected costs, as discussed in Chapter 2. This estimate includes utility setup, soil testing, surveying, and anything to validate that the land is suitable for your needs and within your budget.
10. Buy the land, which we will cover in Chapter 4.

This list may appear daunting, but it is actually much simpler than it looks. You basically need to figure out where you will live in general and then determine which parcels are for sale that fit your needs. Once you identify those parcels, you simply validate that they will work with the zoning department, the budget, and your needs of the land (think utilities connection and soil testing for septic). This process requires patience and research, but you will learn how to navigate quickly. We will dive deep into this shortly..

TYPES OF LAND

When you start your search for land, you will encounter many different types of land, from land advertised as hunting land to recreational land to development sites. The nuance in the type of land makes a difference, as it constitutes land use. Historically, *land use* is closely related to zoning, but not exactly the same. Zoning constitutes how land is divided and what is allowed on those parcels, while land use is more the *intention* and *capability* of the land, both historically and in the future. Often, the intention of the land informs the zoning or vice versa. For example, land designated as commercial rural real estate on a real estate listing will likely have commercial zoning. If you are looking for a place to start a tiny house community, this option may work, but if you are simply looking for a place to put your tiny house residentially, chances are this land is not the right fit, even if the pictures look good and the utility setup matches what you need. Note that land use is not a specific ordinance or even a clearly defined term like zoning. It is simply the relationship between people and the land.

There are various land uses to consider, some of which will support your tiny house needs while others will not.

Residential

If land already includes a residence or is a good fit for a residence, it is considered residential. This type of land use includes land that already has a single-family home, mobile home, tiny home, or cabin. It also includes condos and apartment complexes. In many cases, you will find residential land that does not have a building on it yet. Developers often build communities, investing in the setup of the land so it can be sold to aspiring homeowners wishing to build their dream homes. This approach is certainly an option, especially if your tiny house will be somewhat traditional in its aesthetic and will be on a foundation. Residential land may also have restrictions beyond zoning and building codes, including the types of materials that can be used and whether or not animals are permitted. They also may have HOA fees if you opt for the development route.

The benefit of residential land is that you are allowed to live on it, which removes a lot of hassle. A less clear downside, but a downside all the same, is that the zoning may be a bit rigid with your tiny house. This is the crux of the issue with tiny houses: *they often require residential land but cannot meet its requirements*. But all is not lost! It always comes back to working with your zoning department. You should certainly include residential land in your tiny house land search.

Recreational

Recreational land is designated as such for enjoyment and entertainment. The most famous form of recreational land is a national park. Many other forms of recreational public land exist, from state-owned hunting land to city parks and beaches. However, private land can also be designated as recreational, which include private hunting land, campgrounds, fishing properties, ATV and dirtbike land, and land for horseback riding and hiking.

So can I use recreational land for my tiny house? Maybe. The answer will come down to two main factors. The first is whether or not the land is suitable for living. For example, you may find a nice parcel of hunting land that is too swampy to actually construct a home. The second is whether or not the zoning board will allow for recreational land to be used residentially. Depending on your circumstances, you may get approved, get approved with a special-use permit, or simply get rejected.

The key here is not to assume that land that looks good for a tiny house will automatically allow a tiny house. Even though the land is sometimes advertised as residential, it doesn't mean it is. You may find land on a popular land listing website that says, "build your perfect hunting cabin in the woods." Just because the listing says this does not mean you are allowed to build a hunting cabin. It is implied that you–not the seller or real estate agent–will do your due diligence to ensure the land use and zoning suit your needs.

Agricultural

Any land that is used for the development of crops or livestock is typically designated agricultural. This type of land use can include standard crop farms, home-steads, hobby farms, chicken farms, bee farms, fish farms, ranches, and vineyards. If the land produces food, it is almost certainly agricultural.

Regarding placing or building a tiny house on the land, agricultural land may or may not be suitable. If you are looking at buying a farm that has a house on it, then clearly, humans have been able to live on this land. If you are looking at land that has always been used for industrial-scale farming, you may not be able to use the land for a tiny house, whether that is due to zoning or simply because the land is not suitable for human residence.

Commercial

Land that is used for producing income in a non-agricultural way is typically considered commercial. Commercial land is used or zoned for retail, hotels, offices, factories and plants, hospitals, storage facilities, and many other types of businesses. While purely commercial land is not likely to fit your needs, mixed-use land with a commercial component may. The main exception to this rule is if you are looking to start a tiny house business in the form of a community. You may be able to work with the local zoning department to turn commercial land into a multi-residence property. Work with the zoning board and be thoughtful about how you would use the land.

Transport

You are unlikely to consider this land use, as it is almost entirely owned by government entities and deals with the movement of people and goods. Airports, trains, pipelines, rivers, and roads all fall under transport land use. While you are unlikely to buy a private airport and put your tiny house on the land, you may still interact with transport land use and should at least consider it. Mainly, you should consider if any of the aforementioned types of structures are nearby and if they affect the land you buy. For example, the government may have a right to place a pipeline through your property if there is a fracking site nearby, or the local airport may have the right to fly over your land. Simply put, be cognizant of transport land use but don't consider it for your actual land purchase.

Mixed Use Land

Some areas have designated land for multiple uses, which can be quite exciting for someone looking to not just find a home but also pick up a hobby or start a business. One type is a residential property with a small business, such as a bed and breakfast. Another type is hunting land with farmland onsite.

One more recent type of mixed use designation is that of *agri-tourism*, which is typically a way to boost a rural economy by drawing tourists to its land. This type of land is a mix of various types of land use and typically has requirements from the local zoning ordinance as to how it must be used. Examples of agri-tourism may include wineries with a tasting room, pick-it-yourself pumpkin patches and apple orchards, petting zoos, and ranches where visitors can stay in a lodge onsite. In all of these examples, the land is being used for agriculture and commerce. They may also have residential designation if the owner or visitors can stay onsite. If you are looking to not just find land for your tiny house but also want to create some sort of business out of your endeavor, agri-tourism land use designation is what you should seek.

Mixed land use can be great for aspiring tiny house owners, because the land is typically zoned with flexibility in mind. Land that has always had a unique relationship with the people using it will likely be treated that way moving forward. Don't be surprised if you need to go through a special permit process or if you need to meet certain requirements to retain that permit, but generally, mixed land is a good sign. Work with your zoning department to see how mixed land can work for you.

ZONING

While we may have covered the basics of zoning earlier, we didn't get too deep into it. Now that you have a better sense of the rest of the process, it is time to demystify zoning and understand fully not just what it is but how to deal with it. To say that zoning is a challenge would ultimately be an understatement. It is oftentimes the barrier that prevents people from living tiny. It makes people cringe and get scared. It may be the main reason you found yourself reading this book.

In my time dealing with the practical side of tiny house living, I have spent countless hours decoding the tiny house zoning debacle, helping others by guiding them along the process, or doing zoning research on their behalf. What I will outline here will explain zoning and how to approach it so you can navigate its murky waters. It *is* something that you can overcome or even use to your advantage; you just need the right mindset and approach.

What is Zoning, and Why Does It Exist?

As mentioned earlier, zoning is the collective decision of a municipality, city, or county to control how land and property are used. It is the process of physically dividing the land into parcels, regulating how each of those parcels can be used, cannot be used, and can be used under certain circumstances with zoning board approval. This identification of parcels is achieved by categorizing each parcel into types of land, such as *single-family residential* or *industrial.*

Zoning laws began showing up in the United States in the early 1900s as major cities started to seek ways to prevent development from disrupting neighborhoods and the quality of life, as well as the home value, of their residents. This time period was marked by residential neighborhoods of New York having skyscrapers erected in the middle of their community, urban and suburban areas seeing power plants popping up next to their schools, and runaway development due to the industrial boom. At this time, no zoning existed, and for that reason, residents of these communities had no recourse. If you lived next to a farm, and that farm was turned into a wastewater treatment plant, tough luck!

These situations were met with resistance by local residents in the form of local laws that would become what we now call *zoning.* The most notable case was that of Euclid vs Ambler Realty, which went all the way to the US Supreme Court in 1926. The village of Euclid, Ohio, right outside of Cleveland, denied Ambler Realty the right to build industrial facilities on land in the village. The US Supreme Court ultimately voted in favor of

Euclid, setting the precedent that towns had the right to choose how the land was used in the community.

After this monumental decision, similar regulations began forming rapidly across the United States. And thus, zoning was born.

Despite the well-intended and functionally important origins of zoning, these regulations have no doubt become somewhat dysfunctional or, at the very least, overly complicated. Almost all cities, counties, provinces, towns, and boroughs have zoning, including land that does not have its own municipal government. Due to the local nature of zoning, it is nearly impossible to search "zoning laws in XYZ area" and get results that tell you exactly what you want to know. No such database exists. Zoning is fundamentally decentralized, at least in the United States, Canada, and Australia. For example, North Carolina, a notably tiny house-friendly state, still has 100 counties and over 550 municipalities, meaning there are over 650 different zoning ordinances in the state. Within North Carolina, the city of Charlotte has its own zoning, the county of Henderson has its own zoning, and the town of Brevard has its own zoning. This vast array of ordinances is normal.

Now, this complexity is no doubt daunting, and we could certainly spend all day discussing the good and bad of zoning from a philosophical perspective.

However—we will do no such thing since it does not help you get any closer to your goal of finding land for your tiny house. Instead, it is best that we simply understand that zoning is there for a reason, and it serves a purpose. We cannot change this, but we can choose to understand it and work with it rather than ignore or resent it and put ourselves at risk.

Who Determines and Enforces Zoning?

As mentioned and suggested throughout, zoning is typically decentralized for those seeking a tiny house. If you live in a European country like Germany or France, zoning is controlled mostly or entirely on a national level, so the question of what you can do with your land is much more cut and dry. While this situation is easier to navigate, it actually makes finding land more challenging because the national zoning ordinance gives aspiring tiny house owners a sweeping "yes" or "no" answer. When you get that rejection, there is not much else you can do.

In many countries where the tiny house movement is booming, like the US, Canada, Australia, New Zealand, and the UK, zoning is determined locally. In fact, the UK goes even further than to use zoning, which they technically don't have. Instead, almost all development must go through the local council. In zoning terms, the

British system is akin to having all land zoned with special use permits.

The often misunderstood element about the localized zoning model is that, while it may be seemingly impossible to navigate, it is the greatest advantage of a tiny house owner. With distinct zoning in so many different places, you can find a place with zoning that works for you. Localized zoning—for all its flaws—gives you flexibility!

Regarding the enforcement of zoning, there are a few things to keep in mind. For one, zoning is enforced most often due to a complaint from a neighbor. That phone call or email triggers the zoning or planning department to send an inspector to the house, which can lead to code enforcement. This enforcement on a response-only basis is the norm in most rural areas and many urban and suburban areas. It is typically why many people are comfortable going around the zoning ordinance. They imagine that as long as they are good neighbors or are out of sight and out of mind, they will be fine. In many cases, they are correct. While the risk of inspection is lower, the consequence should you get caught skirting zoning is no less severe.

In the event that zoning does get enforced, a few different things may happen next. The best case scenario is that the zoning board allows the tiny house owner to apply for a special use permit, which would make their living situation compliant with local regulations. A more disruptive and costly scenario is that the zoning board requires the tiny house owner to make changes to the house or property so that it fits into the zoning ordinance. Both outcomes may incur a fine of several hundred dollars, typically after an initial grace period to make the needed changes.

You may wonder: *what if I think my tiny house is within the zoning ordinance? Can I fight back?* The answer is that yes, you can fight the zoning department, but consider what this really means. You are fighting the local government. Be prepared to spend a lot of time and even money with a lawyer to make your case. Know that the local government holds all the cards, and even if you make a strong case for yourself, you will still be at their mercy. The stories of tiny house owners who get on the wrong side of zoning departments are quite scary, including people receiving large fines, notices to vacate their property, and court proceedings. Whatever route you take, know what the worst-case scenario is.

If you choose to find land properly zoned for your needs, there is a specific process that you can take. Here are your step-by-step instructions for finding that perfect parcel!

1) Identify the general area

This step may seem obvious or repetitive, but identifying the general area and *why* you want to live there is crucial.

I work with many people to help them identify viable land and navigate zoning. Frequently, the first thing they tell me is that they want to live in a specific state in the US, to which I ask them, "well, why do you want to live there?"

Sometimes they give a good reason like *I hear that the state is tiny house friendly* or *I am from the center of the state, far from any other, and all of my family is there.*

Other times, they give reasons that restrict them unnecessarily. For example, you may want to place a tiny house in Utah because you like the desert. Yet you can just as easily put a tiny house in the desert of New Mexico or Arizona. If there is nothing actively tying you to the state or province, but rather you are simply associating the state with something you like, break that association and look for the specific environment.

Once you have done this simple step of asking *why* you can start identifying *where.* Use a map of your choosing to identify areas where you may want to live. There is no need to be picky about anything yet, as you are simply trying to identify places you would be willing to live rather than places you will be able to find land.

Your end result may be one solid area, such as the Northern Rockies in western Montana, western Wyoming, and eastern Idaho. It may instead be a collection of multiple areas, such as an area on the coast of Maine plus an area on the coast of Nova Scotia. And, of course, for those of you tied to a specific area for work or family obligations, you already know where you will need to look. While these examples are based in North America, the same logic applies to those living in other parts of the world: find the areas that provide the life you want rather than try to force the life you want into a specific area.

2) Identify the counties and municipalities of your target area

Now that the map is complete, the next step is to identify the local municipalities and counties of your given area because that is how we will identify zoning. Generally speaking, it is best to simply look up the counties. In the past, Google Earth had county lines displayed, but that feature no longer exists. Some tools do exist that overlay county lines onto online maps. A quick internet search will reveal what you need. Likewise, you can simply compare your map of regions with a map of county boundaries.

You will now have your list of the counties you need to research. In your research, you will also identify any municipalities such as towns, townships, boroughs, and cities, which fundamentally are the same as counties in the context of zoning.

Using your list, find the following information for each county:

- **Zoning department website**: this should end with a .gov or .org and will probably look antiquated like most local government websites. However, these websites are where you should start, as they often have the information you need. It is in your best interest to google "XYZ County zoning department," and the first result is probably what you need. You can also simply search for the local government website and then navigate to the zoning department page. Generally, you can learn a lot about the local government structure and zoning board by spending ten minutes clicking around.
- **Zoning department contact:** there is likely a *contact* section or simply a phone number and email at the bottom of the page. Write these down.

- **Zoning board members:** you may be able to find information about who you will be dealing with and what their roles are. It can be helpful to have their names so that you can more easily figure out who you are speaking to when you call. This information may not be available, and that is ok. It is simply nice to have.

- **Zoning ordinance:** the zoning ordinance, sometimes simply a table, is the zoning law itself. There is no way to know the zoning without looking at this table; even if you call the zoning office, they will refer you to this table. The ordinance can be found on the zoning website, though if you're having issues finding it, the zoning department will certainly provide it. The goal in finding the ordinance is not for you to read every piece of local government legislation but to find the tables that identify how different categories of parcels can be used. The ordinance is your key to identifying what type of land in a municipality is viable for your tiny house need. We will unpack how to do this in the next section, but for now, understand that you need access to the ordinance.

- **Zoning map:** the goal here is to identify municipalities within the county. For example, you may find that the county has a town or two within it with its own zoning ordinances, but the rest of the county adheres to the county zoning ordinance. In a handful of states, you will find townships, which may fully divide the county into subdivisions, each with its own zoning ordinance. If you're lucky, the county will just have a county ordinance, and that is it. The second objective is to find the parcel viewer, which is typically called GIS. Often the website has a GIS section that you can click and find a link to this interactive GIS map. This is how we identify the parcels in a particular place, at least in the United States. The GIS map also sometimes has the zoning identifier attached to the parcel, which is then used to cross-reference the zoning ordinance. We will break down how to navigate these maps, but for now understand that this is something you need to find, even if it is as rudimentary as a PDF image of the map.

3) Understand the zoning ordinance

Understanding the zoning ordinance is key, specifically the permitted uses in the document. When you find the document, first search the document or page for the word *tiny house* or *tiny home*. If you are looking to put on ADU on land you already have, then search the page for *ADU* or *Accessory*. This search is just a shortcut to see if the ordinance has any specific language around tiny houses.

More often than not, the county will not have tiny house language written into the ordinance, but that does not mean you cannot place or build a tiny house. Instead, you need to next find the permitted use section, typically within a section called *Use Regulations* or *Permitted Use* or *Land Use*. Essentially, it is the section of the ordinance that tells you what you can do with specific types of land.

Typically, this section has permitted use tables, which help to identify how each type of land parcel–usually called the zoning district–is allowed to be used. First, find the table key, which shows the letters used to classify land use as being permitted, permitted with a permit, or not permitted. Here are two examples of a permitted use table key:

Example 1:

Key to Table of Permitted Uses
P = Permitted
P* = Permitted with an Administrative Permit
C = Conditional Use Permit
^All uses not listed are prohibited

Example 2:

KEY: (P) Permitted; (S) Permitted with special use permit; (–) not permitted

Note that each key is different in both its format and language but outlines the same yes, no, and maybe of parcels. The *conditional use* and *special use* permit in each key are effectively the same thing; you might be able to use the parcel but need permission first.

Once you know the key to the tables, you can look at the tables themselves. Look through all of it, but focus on the area marked for residential use. The table typically consists of rows that are made up of the permitted use, columns made up of the zoning districts themselves, and the intersection of rows and columns are the permitted use codes from the table key. Here is an example with a key at the bottom as well.

General Use	Zoning Districts									
	AG	RP	CS	RC	E	SE	SM	CR	I	NP
Agricultural										
Agricultural	P	P	P	S	P	S	S	P	P	S
Clearing	P	P	P	S	P	P	P	P	P	P
Kennels	P	P	P	S	S	S	N	S	P	N
Stables (Commercial)	P	P	P	N	P	P	N	N	P	N
Agricultural Accessory Business	S	S	S	S	S	S	S	N	N	S
Residential										
Single-family Dwelling	P	P	P	P	P	P	P	N	N	P
Two-family Dwelling	P	P	P	N	P	P	N	N	P	
Double-wide Mobile Home	P	P	P	P	P	P	P	N	N	P
Single-wide Mobile Home	P	S	P	S	N	S	S	N	N	P**
Conversion Apartment	P	P	P	P	P	P	P	N	N	S
Cluster Development	P	P	P	P	P	P	P	N	N	P
Multi-family	S	N	P	P	N	P	P	S	N	N
Mobile Home Park	S	N	P	P	N	P	P	N	N	N
Commercial Apartment	N	N	N	P	N	N	P	S	N	N
Retirement	N	N	N	N	N	P	N	N	N	N
Family Care Unit	S	S	S	S	S	S	S	N	N	S
Personal Storage	P	P	P	P	P	P	P	N	N	P

Key to Zoning Districts

AG Agricultural	**E** Estate	**CR** Regional Commercial
RP Resource Protection	**SE** Suburban Estate	**I** Industrial
CS Countryside	**SM** Suburban Mixed Use	**NP** Neighborhood Preservation
RC Rural Center		

Key to Table of Permitted Uses:

P = Permitted
S = Special Use Permit
N = Not Permitted
* All uses not listed are prohibted
P** = Permitted in NP Districts with an "MH" designation, or in mobile home parks

We are then seeking land uses that are permitted or may be permitted through a special use permit. From the table above, let's say we are looking to place a single tiny house on wheels. From simply thinking about what a tiny house on wheels is, we identify the following possible land uses from the rows on the left: agricultural, single-family dwelling, double-wide mobile home, and single-wide mobile home. From these four possible uses, we can see the following zoning districts that might suit us.

For example, the single-wide mobile home option is permitted in the AG (Agricultural) and CS (Country-side) zoning districts, while it is permitted under special use permits for the RP (Resource Protection), RC (Rural Center), SE (Suburban Estate), and SM (Sub-urban Mixed Use) zoning districts.

Now, it is important to note that you cannot simply claim your tiny house as a single-wide trailer and then put it on this land. You will need to work with the zoning department to classify your tiny house. Luckily, you now have the information you need to have that conversation.

4) Call the zoning department

You now have the zoning tables figured out, or at least understand what it is. You can give the zoning depart-ment a call. Since you have digested the zoning ordi-nance, your call with them will be much more fruitful. You can ask them about specific zoning districts, and specific land uses from the table. Zoning department staff appreciate it when you have more information and a bit of background on the zoning ordinance. More importantly, they can help you much more if you ask specific questions.

When you call the zoning department, talk to them openly about your plans. Tell them that you want to build or place a tiny house and what kind of tiny house it is. Don't assume that the zoning department knows what you mean when you say "tiny house." In your conversation, mention that you have seen the zoning ordinance and want to understand how your tiny house plans fit into it.

The individuals within the zoning department are there specifically for these conversations, so they are typically helpful and reasonable.

If your conversation goes in the direction of rejection, ask the zoning department individual if there is any way that you can have a tiny house in the municipality. If the answer is a clear "no," then cross this area off your list and ask them if they know of any nearby counties or municipalities that are more friendly to tiny houses.

If the answer is that you can live in a tiny house in certain zoning districts, then ask the zoning department individual to email you the summary of that zoning rule. For one, it will help you keep your research in order. If you reach out to ten different zoning departments, you will quickly forget the rules of each municipality. Secondly, you will want to have documentation of your discussion in writing. Since zoning department approval will be the first step in launching your tiny house project, you want their written word that you will be able to get approval and how.

There is a good chance that the zoning department will forward you to the planning department. In this case, make that phone call and do the same due diligence with the planning department.

The ultimate goal of these phone calls is to have written confirmation that you have a way to live in a tiny house legally and a clear understanding of what must occur to do so. With these two tasks complete, you will know not only that you can look for land, but which type of land will suit your tiny house needs.

5) Cross reference the GIS maps with the zoning ordinance

While steps 4 and 5 are likely happening in tandem, a large amount of research will likely come after you have a clear grasp of the zoning ordinance. The goal of looking at the GIS parcel viewer is to identify parcels of land that are zoned in a way that will suit your tiny house.

Using the example table from above, let's say that your call with the zoning department revealed that your tiny house on wheels would require a special permit but can be placed in the following zoning districts: AG (Agriculture), RP (Rural Protection), and CS (Countryside).

Your next task is to look at the GIS map and find these specific zoning districts within the county or municipality. When you get to the GIS map, you will need to turn on the *zoning* layer of the map, which is done through the menu in the top right or top left. A well-made and accessible GIS map will have this zoning layer available, enabling you to click on a given parcel and see its zoning district. Alternatively, the zoning district may be overlaid on the map itself.

Here is an example of a GIS map. As you can see, the zoning layer is selected, the map displays each parcel, and each parcel has an associated planning and zoning code.

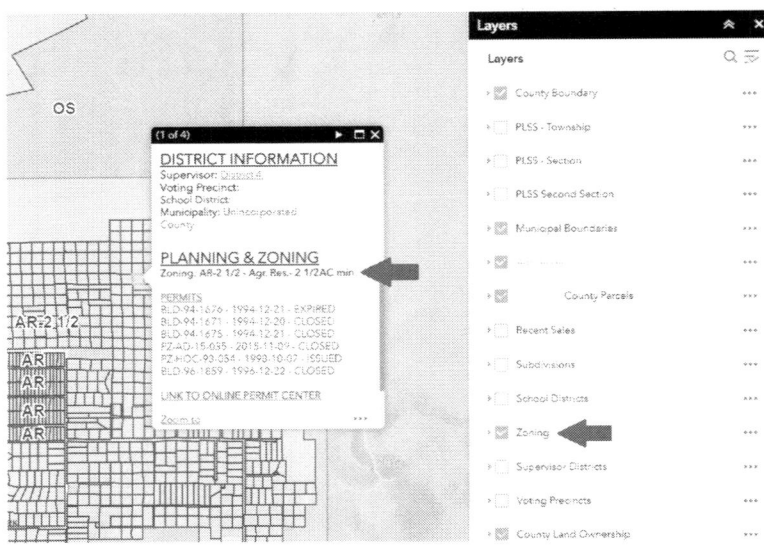

Sample Interactive GIS Map

While the map above is what you can hope for, the truth is: most counties have an imperfect GIS map that fails to include zoning. In some places, GIS has not even been implemented, and thus the zoning map is simply a PDF of the municipality map, color-coded to each zoning district. In either case, you will need to be resourceful. Use the address to find the parcel on the image of the map, or contact the zoning department and ask where you can find a parcel map that shows zoning.

Once you have identified the parcels that will fit your needs, you can now begin to search for the property you can buy among those parcels. When you find parcels for sale, be sure to confirm with the zoning department once again that the parcel is zoned properly. The GIS map is not always 100% accurate, and most zoning departments recommend you use it for research but not for confirmation.

6) Repeat

Once you do this process for one county or municipality, move on to the next. At first, the process is a bit intimidating, but after your first time going through the process of finding the ordinance, calling the zoning department, and finding parcels on the GIS map, you will be able to move through the process quite quickly.

If this process sounds way too difficult, scary, or time-consuming, you have a couple of options to outsource it. For one, since this process requires a bit of online navigation, get help from a friend or family member to go through the process with you if you are not very tech-savvy. Generally speaking, this process will feel less daunting if you approach it with someone else. Additionally, you can rely on your real estate agent to an extent, especially if you have narrowed your search down to a relatively specific area, but remember that their goal is for you to buy land and not necessarily to make sure you buy the perfect parcel of land. If you want some or all of the research done for you, you can contact us at TinyHousePractical.com.

Unrestricted Land

The holy grail of finding land for your tiny house is finding land that has no restrictions. It does exist, but it isn't easy to find. Typically, zoning-free land is in not just rural but truly isolated areas. This setup is perfect for those seeking an off-grid refuge, as long as they are not too concerned with the isolation and relative difficulty of living far from town.

You should also consider that unrestricted land isn't a whole lot different from land that is only somewhat restricted. For example, you may find land that allows tiny homes and septic system installation but restrict drilling a well. If you don't need a well, you have a parcel you can use here; but if you are looking only for the magical 'unrestricted land,' you will unnecessarily skip this piece of land.

Another consideration regarding unrestricted land is that you will typically have unrestricted land surrounding you. That means you can do what you want with your parcel, as can the neighbors with their parcels.

Nevertheless, unrestricted land is an excellent option for tiny houses. The real question is: how do you find such land? We all wish there were a map of unrestricted land at our disposal, ready to tell us exactly where to look, but that isn't the case. Finding unrestricted land requires substantial research and will be out of the question for many whose desired regions simply have none. Land is sometimes listed as unrestricted but isn't actually unrestricted.

To begin your search, narrow down the locations where you're willing to live, and then start discussing with a real estate agent or a municipality in the area. Unrestricted land doesn't fall under the jurisdiction of the zoning department because there isn't one if the land has no restrictions. That means you will need to go to the websites of counties in rural areas and contact someone from their administrative office.

HOW TO ANALYZE THE LAND

Now that you understand the types of land, it's time to understand what to look for when you analyze the land. This analysis is fundamental in the land search and purchasing process. It includes not just how the land looks and feels but also how it can be used and accessed.

First, consider the basic criteria of the land to rule out irrelevant parcels. Price, zoning, and location are the most obvious factors. If any of the three don't meet your criteria, then you can move on to the next parcel. For efficiency in your search, focus on these factors first. For off-market searches, you don't know the price but can estimate it based on real estate records and nearby properties for sale.

Once you have identified parcels that meet the price, zoning, and location criteria, you should consider the level to which the land is developed. As previously discussed in the *Financials* section, land may be completely unimproved, ready for a home, or somewhere in between. While listings typically say whether or not the land is raw, unimproved, or improved, you should think beyond the general label. Instead, focus on the following elements.

- **Electricity:** The electricity setup is occasionally listed within the body of the listing. If it is not, that might indicate that electricity is not set up, but not necessarily. Sometimes photos of the listing include electrical meters and power lines, which indicate that electricity won't be an issue. You will need to contact the local power company to understand how accessible electricity is to the property and, if there is setup to be done, how much it will cost. If you are going the off-grid solar route, you can ignore the electrical setup, but make sure that you have calculated how much solar power you will need and that there is enough shadeless space to meet your power demand.

- **Natural gas:** Many rural tiny house owners, both fixed and on wheels, don't bother with a natural gas hookup and instead use their own propane tanks to support their gas needs and electrical backup needs. This decision is discussed extensively in my book *How to Build a Tiny House on Wheels Step by Step.* Nevertheless, consider how readily available natural gas lines are to your home if you are living in a suburban or urban area or simply don't want to deal with refilling propane tanks. Listings often identify whether or not natural gas is set up on the land.

For those that plan to use wood power instead, check with the local government to see if there are burning limits.

- **Sewer**: For the nomadic tiny house owner, off-grid waste management will be your best bet, using a composting toilet or similar. For those that are staying put, you may want to have a proper sewage system. Some parcels may have this already connected, while others may have the ability to connect it. Depending on the municipality and your proximity to the municipal sewer lines, connecting to sewage may or may not be feasible. Some municipalities will connect you for free or little cost, while others may require that you cover the expensive process of laying pipes from a faraway sewer line. To know for sure, inquire with the local utility department. If connecting to sewage is not an option, your first fallback option is septic. To validate that the land can accommodate septic, it must pass a soil test or perc test, as previously mentioned. If you buy land that fails a perc test and can't connect to sewage, you will need to set up off-grid non-septic sewage.

- **Water**: Similar to sewage, water requires a municipal connection for those opting to go on-grid, which may be free, cheap, or costly. The same guidance applies: talk to your local utilities department. If you will be setting up off-grid water, you should consider the most popular option, a well. To evaluate whether or not you can have a well, you need to confirm with the zoning or utilities department whether or not you are allowed to install a well at all, and if so, what permits are required. Then, get a well-drilling company to evaluate the land to understand if a well is possible and how deep it must go. Some people install their own wells, but even if you choose this option, you need to know how deep it will be and if it is feasible. For example, if you buy land on a mountain peak, you may need to drill through significant layers of rock for hundreds of feet, which can cost over $10,000. When considering a well, you must identify whether it can be drilled and what it will take to get the drilling equipment onto the property. Additionally, you need to understand your water rights or lack thereof. Suppose you intend to source water from the earth, rivers, or skies. In that case, you may be unpleasantly surprised to find out that you are prohibited from doing so, or at least restricted in how you do so, such as being limited on the volume of rainwater you can collect. For those living in dry or heavily irrigated areas, which includes most of the western United States, you can expect this to be a major topic in your land evaluation.

- **Communications**: Internet and telephone may require electricity, but their connection is a separate utility. You don't see the communications information provided on listings all that often, so you will likely need to do your research. While this is not much of an issue for those living in developed areas, those buying raw land in remote areas must do their due diligence. It is not a given that you will have internet or cell phone service easily set up on your land. Contact the local internet service provider (ISP) about broadband, and consider talking to the neighbors (if any exist) to see how they connect. Some options to consider beyond traditional high-speed internet include cellular internet, satellite internet, dial-up, and fixed wireless.

Your land will certainly affect you beyond your utilities. Be sure to consider how much of the land is habitable. This consideration is essential when purchasing raw land or converting land traditionally used for non-residential purposes. Even if the land is habitable, make sure you know exactly where it is habitable. You could find a sizable property, but only a small portion of it is not a swamp. That portion of the land may butt up to the parcel next to yours, meaning you have enough land, but your tiny house is next to your neighbor's. If privacy is what you desire, this setup probably will not work. Another example is buying land on a steep hill. Unless you reform the land or build a tiny house on stilts, you will have to find flat land. For those with a tiny house on wheels, flat land is a must.

You also need to consider the land at all times of the year. Consider the trees on your property. During winter, will they provide adequate privacy? During summer, will they provide adequate shade? Will they impact solar power?

Additionally, consider the hazards. You should avoid a tiny house that is on a floodplain. Most countries with rain have floodplain hazard maps showing the likelihood of flooding. In the United States, the Federal Emergency Management Agency publishes an interactive online flood map that allows you to search for your address or area. You should avoid any flood zone that is deemed to have a 1% chance of annual flooding or worse. These zones are also called 100-year floodplains.

Beyond avoiding flood and considering trees, there are several other factors to consider, including natural disaster likelihood from tornadoes and hurricanes, insect infestation issues, corrosivity from salty air near an ocean, elevation, and the strength of the wind. If you have an existing tiny house, validate that the land can actually handle the elements. If you do not have a tiny house and plan to build it on the land, make sure you intentionally build it to handle the specific climate.

Now that we have confirmed the land will meet our utility needs and accounted for the local climate, it is time to envision the tiny house on the land! Take the map of the land, walk the property if possible, and start to sketch out where you will put the tiny house. Sketch out fences, wells, septic, driveways, trees, gardens, solar arrays, chicken coops, firepits, and anything else that isn't simply the grass or dirt. You should be able to envision your property before you buy. While plenty of people buy the land and figure it out as they go, you can avoid future surprises by doing a bit of planning up front with something as simple as a drawing on a piece of paper.

Once you have sketched your home configuration, your last step is considering access. Will cars, construction vehicles, or delivery services be able to get to your house? Secondly, and often overlooked, will vehicles be *allowed* to get to your house? During your due diligence, you will need to identify any easements on the land. An easement is a legal situation where a person or organization can use another person's property for a specific purpose. The most common easement you will run into is where your driveway runs through another person's land or vice versa. In this situation, one owner is allowed to use the other's land solely to access their own property. With this kind of easement, there may be vehicle size restrictions, so while you're allowed to drive your pickup truck to your house, you may not be allowed to bring in a bulldozer without their permission.

Note that other easements could affect you in different ways, such as easements owned by utility companies to run electric, water, and communication lines. Another easement to consider is that which is tied to mineral rights. It is often not connected to the land itself, but instead is retained by the previous owner or is owned by an energy company. In some cases, this gives them the right to extract the minerals beneath your land, even if it means installing a well on the surface. While this was more of a known issue—or for some lucky landowners, the equivalent of hitting the lottery—back when the fracking boom started, it is something to consider but less of a concern nowadays. Chances are strong that your land will not be drilled or mined if it hasn't already, but you should still consider the possibility.

Ultimately, analyzing land means envisioning each step of the process you will have to take to place or construct your tiny house and then happily live in it. It is easy to see land at the right price with the right zoning and skip straight to the assumption that it is the right parcel. Think methodically through each of the previously mentioned factors and validate that your life will be the one you want on your parcel of land. If you do, you will find the right piece of land for you!

THE RIGHT MINDSET TO ANALYZE LAND

As we wrap up this chapter on searching land and identifying zoning, it is important that you approach this process with patience and determination. The mindset needed to find land for a tiny house is one of flexibility. Unfortunately, finding land will not be easy for the vast majority of locations, but being flexible with your location will greatly improve your chances of finding land.

Likewise, flexibility and collaboration with zoning departments is key. Unless you choose to go under the radar—and accept the risk of doing so—the zoning departments you work with will be your biggest ally. Approach them with partnership in mind.

The key to your search will always come back to the root question: *why do I want to live in a tiny house?* If you can answer this question, then you know your true end goal. If you keep this goal in mind, you will know which sacrifices can and cannot be made.

If you know your motivation and constantly remind yourself of it, you will have the strength and willpower to overcome this challenge.

You will find the land you need to have the life you want.

FINDING & BUYING LAND

You may be thinking: *I now understand how to analyze land, but how do I actually find it?* This is perhaps the most difficult question for many aspiring tiny house owners to answer, but many different methods exist. Before we even dive into the methods, remember that finding land starts with creating a large list of properties that meet three key requirements: location, price, and zoning. These three factors should be considered in your broad search for parcels. Once you have completed your broad search, exhausting your area of all possible parcels, you can then apply the more specific analysis where you consider utilities, land use, construction, and any other pertinent factors.

With this approach in mind, let's unpack the various ways you can find actual parcels of land.

ONLINE

It is recommended that you begin your search online for two reasons. Firstly, it is easy; you can do it from your couch. Secondly, it will educate you quite extensively. Researching land in various areas will give you a great idea of how much you can expect to pay for different sizes of raw, unimproved, and developed land. It will also help you start to internalize the content of this book, knowing it through experience rather than just academically.

To search online, you should look on various real estate websites, some of which are purely focused on land real estate. Here are the names of some listing sites to check out:

- Land.com
- Land and Farm
- Land Watch
- Land Search
- Billy Land
- LoopNet
- Zillow
- Trulia

- ForSaleByOwner.com
- Facebook Marketplace

While finding land online is an option, and certainly where you should begin your search, it does have a few drawbacks. Firstly, anyone can access these listings, which means you will have to act quickly on desirable land. For land that is not desirable, you will typically see how long the listing has been posted on the site. Many parcels of land on these sites are lower-quality; the high-quality parcels often never make it to listing sites. That said, you may find what you need in a parcel of land others don't want since most people aren't looking for land for a tiny house. That is the beauty of a tiny house on wheels or an off-grid cabin.

REAL ESTATE AGENT

You should bring in a land-focused real estate agent at some point in the process, whether it is before you close on a property or early in the process. You can think of them as a consultant that knows the general area, understands the process of buying land, and may have a relationship with local zoning and planning departments. They also typically have a software platform that identifies land for sale, which the real estate agent will actively use to find properties for you. Many people find that having a real estate agent searching for properties helps quite a bit because it allows them to not make a full-time job out of finding land. Plus, the seller of the land typically pays the commission, but a buyer's real estate agent has a legal duty to represent the buyer. This duty includes helping you identify your needs, finding the land, educating you on the process, showing you each property, submitting and negotiating an offer on your behalf, referring you to reliable professionals when needed, making sure insurance is in place, handling due diligence, and more.

When searching for your real estate agent, you can start by tapping into your network. If you have friends and family in the area who have purchased land, have them connect you with the agent they used. If not, you can start by looking at the aforementioned online listings. Most of these listings will have an associated real estate agent. When you see the real estate agent, look them up. Find out what real estate agency or brokerage they work for, and research that business. It is just like hiring a contractor, or any professional for that matter: you should be able to get in touch with them easily, and they should have a good reputation. You should also feel comfortable when you communicate with them. Buying property is a personal process, so your agent should be someone you can trust to help you and listen to you.

LAND AUCTIONS

"Going once...going twice...sold!"

While most people have seen an auction dramatized in a movie or show, many don't know much about them. Cars, storage units, fine art, collectors' items, industrial equipment, and land are all auctionable. If it has value, it can be auctioned. The purpose of an auction is to level the competition and bring transparency to the purchase, which is land in our case. Auctions have an auctioneer (the fast-talking person) who auctions the land on behalf of the seller, typically a bank. Bids on the land are taken in real-time, whether that is in-person, online, or via phone. The person who bids the highest has bought the land.

When a property is put up for auction, it is typically due to foreclosure, tax deeds, or tax liens. Foreclosure occurs when an owner fails to pay the lender over several months, so the lender takes possession of the property. Tax lien auctions are similar, but the government seizes the purchase due to tax fraud or unpaid taxes. Tax lien auctions are the sale of the lien to the highest bidder; the lien owner then has the right to seize the property or collect the owed taxes directly. This sale is a bit nuanced but still results in an auction. The third type, a tax deed sale, is the sale of the property and the unpaid taxes bundled together.

Real estate auctions come in three forms:

- **Absolute auction**: This is an auction where the seller will accept the highest bid, regardless of the price. This is less common.
- **Minimum bid**: This is an auction where the seller sets the minimum price and only accepts offers above that price.
- **Selling with reserve**: This is an auction where the seller has the right to reject any bid. These auctions can lead to you winning the bid but not getting the property, so consider this less of a sure bet.

Real estate auctions have several benefits to the aspiring tiny house owner. For one, there is a commitment to sell and a desire to sell quickly. Banks don't want to own real estate. This means that you won't encounter the frustrating situation of finding land, conducting due diligence, negotiating, and going back and forth with a seller and your respective real estate agents, only to have the seller back out at the last minute. Instead, you will be able to research and conduct due diligence ahead of the sale date, often given to you by the auction house in the form of a due diligence packet. You will confidently know when the land is being sold and then close within 30 days, which is a rapid close time. The acceleration and certainty are big draws to auction-goers.

Additionally, land at auction is often priced fairly or at a bargain because the buyers collectively determine the property's value by bidding what they think is fair. For this reason, you can find land at a discount or at your maximum price, assuming you don't get sucked into the emotional thrill of winning a sale. There is also fair competition since every buyer is armed with the same information and access to the auction. Auctions do not require negotiations. The bank is starting at or below a fair market value, the buyer is starting low, and the winner is the buyer willing to spend the most.

Despite the many advantages of auctions, there are a few downsides to consider. Firstly, if you are impulsive or overly competitive, it is easy to get lost in the moment of trying to win the auction, resulting in paying more than you can afford. Second, auctions require you to be proactive with your research, which means researching the land and dealing with the zoning and building departments as needed. Since auctions occur on a set date, you will have to operate quickly and decisively, answering two key questions: *(1) Will I be able to put my tiny house on this land? (2) What is my maximum budget for the land purchase?* Answering these questions is not always easy without time on your side. Auctions also typically require pre-approval if there is financing involved and require a down payment on the spot to secure your purchase. This scenario can be an issue if you don't have your finances in order. Lastly, you may not have adequate access to the property to really know what you are buying. Auctions often come as-is, meaning that the condition of the property is what it is, take it or leave it. You may have to assume the risk here, but if you can buy property at a steep discount, it may still be worthwhile, especially if you have a clear vision of your budget and what the potential costs may be.

To prepare for an auction, take the following steps:

1. Go to an auction or two as an observer to get a feel for the process.
2. Discuss with your real estate agent.
3. Read and understand all transaction details and due diligence information before the auction.
4. Determine the estimated market value of the land.
5. Drive by the property and inspect it from the outside.

6. Identify the parcel's zoning and discuss your plans with the zoning department. Make sure the land will suit your needs.

7. Ensure you have pre-approval for financing, when applicable, and make sure you have cash available for a deposit.

8. Confirm that the auction is occurring since it isn't uncommon for them to get canceled or postponed.

9. Attend the auction and bid on the land parcel or parcels.

Altogether, auctions are a viable option for finding land for your tiny house. With a little bit of care and focus, you can find discounted property that you simply would not find if you went directly to the seller's market.

OFF-MARKET LAND

Have you ever driven down a country road by a beautiful piece of land, maybe overlooking a valley or nestled by a creek, and said to yourself, "wow, I wish I could have *that* property?" Despite the lack of a *for sale* sign on the property, you still have options to buy that property. Enter the world of off-market land.

Off-market land is land that is not listed on the Multiple Listing Service, which is the engine that public listings go through to get posted.

While finding off-market listings may be difficult and tedious, it is an incredible way to find valuable land. Off-market land may be for sale, but the owner wishes to keep the sale private. It also could be land that is not for sale, but you try to buy it anyway. There is a reason for the saying, "everything is for sale at the right price."

To identify off-market land for sale, first use word of mouth, both in-person and online. When talking to contractors, friends, neighbors, and anyone you know in the area, you should be sharing your plans and simply asking: "do you know anyone that might be interested in selling their land?" Many decades ago, before newspapers and certainly before the internet, this is how most real estate transactions were conducted. It is still a powerful method.

To spread the word online, search Facebook for off-market real estate groups in your area and join tiny house and real estate Facebook groups and Discord channels. Here you may find people selling their land. You also can simply post in these groups that you wish to buy land. Some groups are more useful than others, so be diligent, and you may find a good connection. Just be wary of online scammers looking to take advantage.

An alternative online avenue is to go to off-market real estate listing sites, which you can find by searching "off-market listings in my area" or going to known sites like Zillow and FSBO for their off-market listings. Off-market listings have increased in popularity lately, so there are more online tools like these to find off-market listings. The thing about these marketplaces is that they don't exactly remove competition; in essence, they simply shrink the market. It is like going through the express line at an amusement park; you have a better time than people waiting in the regular line, but you don't exactly have the ride to yourself.

The most valuable avenue to consider is contacting property owners directly, known in the real estate world as *direct marketing*. While this tactic is typically used by real estate investors to find hidden gem properties without any competition, you can and should use it to find properties that meet your tiny house criteria. Unfortunately, public listings that meet zoning ordinances are few and far between.

How to Find Possible Sellers

The most challenging part of finding off-market land is identifying possible sellers, as this process requires significant research. Since zoning is the biggest hurdle, you should always start by identifying which type of land *could* work for you. Once you have done that, it is time to find land that meets those criteria. If you only go on-market, then your options may be limited, but since every parcel–for sale and not for sale–falls into the zoning ordinance, you can create a list of all the land that might be able to support your tiny house.

From here, it is time to narrow down those properties based on your specific criteria. That firstly means filtering out land that is likely out of your price range. If you have a $40,000 budget for land purchase but find a 500-acre improved land property, you aren't going to be able to offer a price that is even close to affordable for the land, so you might as well cut that parcel from the list. You also should filter out based on any other criteria that matter to you. That could be the type of land, how raw or improved it is, whether the land already has a house, its school district, or simply the google street view look of the place.

It is also worthwhile to drive around the area to better correlate the zoning map to the county. You might find land that looks good on paper but is unsuitable based on the look and feel. Additionally, you may find land advertised for sale via a physical poster.

Once you have a list of the parcels, it is time to figure out who owns the property. There are many different ways to find the owner:

1. **Check public records:** Your first step should be going online and simply searching *[Your County or Municipality] property search.* In many cases, this will bring you to a page from the local government website that allows you to search the database for ownership. It may be run by the assessor's office, the county clerk, or even the local library. In most cases, you will need either the home address or the parcel ID, found from the GIS map or, if need be, by identifying the parcel on Google Maps. If you still can't find the property search, give your contact in the zoning department a call. They will know what you need to do to access the public record, whether online or in a physical office.

2. **Use search tools:** There are many tools nowadays for finding information based on address. These tools range in quality and cost, but their ultimate goal is to help you do online detective work when trying to connect land to a person. While you shouldn't expect these tools to magically give you a list of all the numbers you need, you can anticipate having some extra leads if the public record search doesn't work out. A few of today's most popular options that allow you to search by name or address include

Spokeo, TopConnector, Intelius, Property Shark, and PeopleSmart.

3. **Talk to a title company:** A title company typically helps later in the buying process. They identify the owner of the land, as well as any issues the property may have. These issues include outstanding mortgages or debts, existing liens, unpaid HOA fees, transfer of ownership restrictions, easements, and leases. While this full service will cost you a few hundred dollars and is better saved for specific properties, many title companies also offer cheap or free real estate lead lists. Search for title companies in your area and get in contact with them.

4. **Go to the property:** Even though it is unlikely to show up to a vacant parcel of land to find the owner, it is still worthwhile. For one, there may be some sort of poster or sign with contact information. The land also may have neighbors who know the owner and have their contact information. Just put on your detective hat!

How to Contact Possible Sellers

Once your list is narrowed down and you have the land owner's contact information, it is time to start contacting them by whichever means you have. If you have their home address, send them a letter. If you have their phone number, give them a call. If you have their email, send them an email.

The key here is to be creative, genuine, and clear. Creativity plays a key role if you cannot contact them directly at their phone number. Creativity is not about being artsy or silly, but merely about getting their attention. An email should have a title that grabs their attention and doesn't look like a marketing email. A letter to them should be hand-written both in the letter and on the envelope, and should not look like a marketing campaign since people often throw those in the trash without looking at them. You want the person to open your mail and read it.

That leads to the importance of being genuine. You are asking someone to sell their land that is not for sale. If you received a letter from a stranger offering to buy your current house, would you be more likely to follow up with them if they sounded formal and vague, or if they explained to you who they are and why they want your house? I'd bet it's the latter because it is easier to trust the person and their intentions when they are open.

Lastly, being clear is important. While you do want to share a little bit about yourself and your intentions for the land, you should not write a novel and you need to have a clear proposal. Do your research on the area and determine a fair price per acre (or hectare) for their type of land, then offer them that amount. Don't offer them above what you are willing to pay or can afford. If you cannot make a fair offer yet, then say so. Be specific about where the parcel of land is, in case they own multiple parcels. Finally, make sure you give them a phone number and return address.

Here is a sample of a hand-written letter that will do the job:

> Dear Devon,
> I noticed that you own 20 acres of land on Green Mountain Road near Norman, Arkansas. My partner Blake and I are originally from Northwest Arkansas and have been living in nearby Dallas for a few years. We are searching for land in the mountains to build a tiny house and raise a family. Your property looks perfect for us. We especially love that there is a creek in the back for our future kids to explore.
>
> We would like to buy your land if you're willing to sell it. We're willing to pay $2300 per acre, $46,000 total.
>
> Would you be interested in selling the land? If so, please contact me at 479-123-4567 or email me at TinyHousePractical.com.

Sincerely,
Jordan Liberata

This sample letter is creative because it is handwritten (yes, that's all it takes). It is genuine because it explains the who, what, and why of the letter. The letter is also clear because it gives a direct proposal, asks a direct question, and asks the recipient to follow up via phone or email. Follow these guidelines and you have a good shot at finding off-market land.

Now you may be wondering, *what should I do if the owner doesn't get back to me?* In this case, not all hope is lost. For one, they may never have received your letter or email, so try to get into contact with them in a different way. The more direct your contact is, the better. Don't bombard them with messages, but do be persistent. Think about how you would feel if a stranger contacted you in multiple ways in rapid succession. Most people find this annoying, if not unsettling. That said, don't just write a letter and then give up when you don't hear. Some people need a little finesse, so if a week or two goes by with no response, reach out again. Never act annoyed that they didn't respond; be gracious and kind. For one, they don't owe you a response, but more importantly, having a positive attitude will make them more likely to sell their land and will make the transaction smoother should they accept.

From researching the land to contacting its owner, you should now understand the off-market approach. While this method is not easy, it is the most likely way for you to overcome the hurdle that likely led you to this book in the first place: the fact that land is so tough to find for a tiny house. If you are committed to overcoming this barrier no matter what, off-market properties is your golden ticket.

WAYS TO FIND LAND TO RENT

Finding land to rent is similar to finding land for sale. It is an excellent option if you newly live in a tiny house on wheels, if you are unsure where you want to live, if you simply can't afford to buy the land you desire, or if you want to avoid the land-buying process.

If you are looking for land to rent that is already set up for a tiny house on wheels, you should look into RV parks, mobile home parks, and tiny house villages. Of course, these options mean you have neighbors with you. To some, the community feel is a big appeal. To others, it defeats the purpose. If you aren't sure, search for some in your area and check them out. They come in many forms; some are rundown and cramped, while others are upscale and spacious. Just keep in mind that for many of these villages, your tiny house must be RVIA or NOAH certified.

If the tiny house village approach isn't appealing, you will need to find private land to rent. There are passive and active ways to find this type of rentable land. The more passive route is to search for existing land rentals on local listing sites like Craigslist, Facebook, and Nextdoor, as well as tiny house-specific sites like Park-MyBnb.com and TryItTiny.com. Many have luck with sites that connect farms with people who can work in exchange for room and board as well, such as WOOF and WorkAway, but these gigs typically already provide housing, so you will need to make special arrangements to the host for bringing your tiny house onsite. You can also post to many of the various sites listed here, advertising that you are seeking land. The main challenge with the "search, post, and wait" approach is that you and a landowner must be on the same website in the location you need. Additionally, many of these landowners are asking for exceptionally high rent. They know their land is valuable and want to earn from it. While there is nothing inherently wrong with this, it can make your search challenging, eliminating many parcels that simply don't make financial sense.

Much like searching for land to buy, the more active and personal approach to finding land can be much more fruitful. First, identify the area where you want to reside. Second, use the same approach used to buy land, where you use the online parcel map or GIS map to identify suitable parcels. Then track down the owner of those parcels, and do your best to contact them personally. Many people own land and have no idea that tiny houses on wheels exist, so they may not even know that they have suitable land for a tenant.

An even more local and personal approach is to go door to door among the parcels that you have identified as possible places to rent. The wonderful thing about renting is that you don't have to find land with no house. Many large properties with one house may have space for you to live completely out of sight of them and out of sight of the road. Additionally, your house may qualify as an ADU, so you can actually live on the property in a way that complies with the zoning ordinance. Even if the property is not zoned for an ADU or a tiny house in general, the landowner may not care. This scenario still invites the risk that the zoning department or landowner demands you leave, but it comes with much less consequence since you are not financially tied to the land.

Altogether, finding land is a matter of persistence and flexibility. By being flexible, you ensure that you find an area that meets your personal needs while also fitting with the zoning needs of tiny houses. But more than anything, you need to be persistent. Keep doing research, making phone calls, and sending letters. Simply commit to the vision that you will find a way to have a tiny house. With this mentality, you are unstoppable.

BUYING LAND

Once you have finally found your parcel and confirmed that the zoning will work for your specific needs, it is time to buy the land itself. This process is best done with a real estate agent specializing in raw land. The exception to this rule is if you are either already experienced in land purchasing or buying land for less than $5,000, in which case you may benefit from simply hiring a real estate attorney to ensure the legal documents involved are legitimate. Regardless of whether or not you use an agent, you will benefit from knowing what to expect throughout this five-step process.

Step 1: Find Land

Luckily, if you are at the point that you are ready to buy a parcel of land, this step is already covered. Now it is time to purchase the land.

Step 2: Negotiate, Make an Offer, & Secure Financing

While negotiating will come before making an offer, securing your financing may happen before or after the negotiation and offer stage, as it depends on the type of financing you use and the terms of the lender.

Before you simply make an offer, it is important to negotiate with the land seller. The list price on land with no structure is often simply a guideline, and if you find the property off-market, no list price exists. That means you should negotiate your offer with the seller. If you find a price that both of you are happy with, it is time to make an offer.

To find a price, you can keep it simple and offer less than you are willing to pay. You can also enlist the help of an appraiser to appraise the land, though that can cost several hundred dollars or more.

Submit a written offer to the buyer, agreeing to a purchase price, any conditions that must be met before finalizing the sale, and the timeline to meet those conditions. This process is known as *due diligence*, which is the next step. If you have a real estate agent, they will create the offer for you. If not, consider getting a real estate attorney to draft the contractual terms of the offer, which also may be referred to as the purchase agreement.

Once you and the seller have signed the offer, it is time to pay *earnest money*. Earnest money is the assurance that you will buy the land if the purchase agreement's conditions are met. It is typically 1-5% of the agreed price of the land. If the land does meet the conditions and you back out of the deal, the seller keeps the earnest money. In essence, the earnest money is a deposit and typically goes toward the final sale. Make sure that your earnest money is not given directly to the seller but is instead placed in an escrow account with escrow services, ensuring that earnest money is properly released.

Step 3: Due Diligence

The due diligence stage is an important part of the process, as it is your checklist that validates that the land is worth purchasing. Typically, your offer will allow for 30-90 days of due diligence. Fortunately, you will have already done a fair amount of due diligence in your evaluation up to this point. You will have confirmed that the land meets your zoning criteria, that any utilities and easements are suitable for you, that the land is accessible for construction, and that the planning department will be open to your project.

The additional due diligence items that need to be completed, and should be outlined in your offer, include requesting information from the seller, performing a land assessment, and performing a title search.

To request information from the seller, your goal here is to simply find out if there are any fees they pay to a Homeowners Association, if they are currently renting out the property, or if there is any ongoing maintenance. If there is an HOA involved, make sure you obtain any documents that pertain to the covenants, conditions and restrictions, also known as CC&R of the property. This information may outline specific rules around the color and design of the house or your ability to have a garden or homestead. Talk to the HOA directly as well. At this point, you should also do a walkthrough of the property if you have not yet done so. Buying sight unseen is not recommended with undeveloped land.

Secondly, you must perform a title search. The title of the land is the legal ownership of it. For those familiar with a deed, the deed is more or less the physical representation of the title, but it can be imperfect. Hence, a title search is necessary to ensure the proper transfer of ownership to you. A title search is a way to investigate the property's ownership history, validating that the seller actually owns the property and has the right to sell the property. A title search also identifies if anyone else has a claim to the property, as well as liens or judgments against the property. Knowing this information is critical because liens are tied to the property, not the person, which means that you could buy land that a bank has a legal right to claim should someone (the seller or otherwise) not pay back their debts. Effectively, buying land with a lien on it may mean accepting someone else's debt. The title search can be achieved through your real estate agent or directly with a title search company. It typically costs $100-200 and takes anywhere from a few hours to a couple of weeks.

Along with the title search, you should obtain tax information for the property from the county or municipal courthouse, ensuring that you know what taxes you will pay for the property. Additionally, you should receive the seller's disclosure documents, which are required by the state so that the seller cannot hide information about the property. Most disclosures relate to home purchases, such as repair history and water damage history, but some are still relevant to land purchases, such as past boundary disputes or environmental hazards. Check with your local planning department to understand what the seller must disclose.

You will also need to conduct a land assessment. At the very minimum, this should include a professional survey of the land unless the local government has records of a recent survey. The land survey should clearly identify the legal boundaries of the land. You want to make sure that you are paying for a 6-acre property and not a 5.7-acre property, for example. Plus, if you have a dispute regarding the property lines in the future, a survey will resolve the matter quickly.

If you buy land with a home on it, the survey may suffice. If you buy undeveloped land like most tiny house owners, a professional environmental assessment is needed as well. For one, an environmental assessment will ensure your safety when living there. Second, it will mitigate the risk of paying for an unforeseen environmental issue later. In the US, the Environmental Protection Agency (EPA) recommends a Phase I assessment, which includes an engineer's analysis of the land, a search of historical land use, aerial photographs, and neighbor interviews. If the Phase I assessment finds evidence of contamination, a Phase II assessment may be in order.

Additionally, if you are installing a septic system, you will need a soil test. You likely have already done this, but if not, now is the time.

For those sourcing water from the land, test the water for drinkability. If you are on vacant land and sourcing the groundwater through a well, have the water professionally tested.

Once all of the relevant conditions are met, you will have completed your due diligence and are now ready to buy!

Step 4: Complete the Sale

The fundamentals of completing the sale are simple but require precision. To complete the sale and properly receive the title, you need to pay the seller the agreed amount and sign and receive the seller's deed, which is the legal document defining ownership. Simple enough, right? Not really…

The reality is that the deed must be legitimate in the first place, which requires a real estate attorney's eyeballs. Secondly, the transfer of the deed must be legitimate, which requires following county or municipality procedures. Depending on your state, that procedure could simply be notarizing the signatures on the deed. It could be much more complex, requiring one or two witnesses and all involved parties to meet in person at the municipality's registry office where the deed will be recorded, at an attorney's office, or with a notary. A real estate lawyer will understand what must occur in your state or province.

It may be tempting to skip this robotic and bureaucratic process and simply operate on a handshake, but that is ill-advised. The reason these procedures exist is to ensure that the transfer of the property is legitimate. The last thing you want is to pay for land but not legally own it. Should any issues arise in the future, you will likely need to prove that you own the land.

Despite all of the legal intricacies, the process itself is pretty straightforward. You review the deed plus all of the documents covered during due diligence. You then sign the deed and any other documents requiring your signature. Then you hand the seller the check for the agreed amount minus whatever amount is held in escrow services, as that is released to the seller. The seller hands you the original deed and keeps a copy for their records. Make sure you keep a copy of all documents and the original deed in a safe place.

Next, you must record the change of ownership with your county, municipality, or both. This step notifies the local government that you now own this property.

You now own land for your tiny house!

THE IMPORTANCE OF PERSEVERANCE

If you take nothing else away from this chapter, it is that perseverance is really all you need to find the right parcel of land.

The majority of people look online for land, and when they see that nothing is available that fits their needs, they give up. Whether they realize it or not, they have only just begun the search.

But you should not give up here. You should get excited about all the potential land you can find to provide you with your ideal tiny house life. Tap into the help of a real estate agent, go after land auctions, find land that isn't even for sale and make your proposal.

You don't need to have much money to do any of this. You don't need to be an expert in real estate or an expert salesman. You don't need any prior experience.

You just need perseverance.

Let's get out there and not stop until we find that perfect parcel!

BUILDING YOUR TINY HOUSE
TO CODE

With a parcel of land to place the tiny house, much of the hard work is done. Now it is time to build the tiny house yourself, have the tiny house built, or buy a tiny house. Regardless of your approach, all successful and legitimate tiny house projects flow through the building or planning department.

THE PERMIT PROCESS

1. Before you start building, speak to the zoning department again. You will often need a special or conditional use permit for your tiny house. Obtain this before you even begin to go to the building department because this step formally

grants you permission to put your tiny house on it.

2. Since you have already confirmed that you can use the land for your tiny house, it is time to contact the building department and discuss your intentions for the land. This moment should certainly not be the first time you speak with them since you will have already discussed your plans for a tiny house with them when ensuring that the land will suit your tiny house needs. At this point, you confirm what permits are required, what you must provide on the permit application, and how much they cost. The building department will likely require you to get multiple permits, such as a new construction permit, an electrical permit, and a plumbing permit, each with an associated fee.

3. Prepare the permit application. You will likely have to include architectural plans to receive your permit. You may buy these plans online, have an architect design them for you, have a tiny house manufacturer provide them to you, or create them yourself using a design software like Sketchup.

4. Submit the permit application and pay the fee for each permit required. The building department will then give you the permits. Be

sure to ask how the building department requires the permits to be displayed. Make sure you also understand when inspections are needed during construction. It is not uncommon for building departments to require inspection at a specific point in the build, such as after the electricity is roughed in, in addition to the final inspection upon completion of the project.

5. Display the permits as instructed, typically visible on the construction site itself.

6. Build your tiny house and get inspections at the checkpoints laid out in the permit. Complete any changes the inspector requires and then have them return to clear you to move on. Once the inspector approves the final build, you are in the clear!

What if I'm not building my tiny house?

Many of these steps are only applicable to those building a tiny house. If you are simply buying a tiny house, you will not need to go through the process of building permits, but you will still need the approval of the building department or the zoning department. Typically, a purchased tiny house requires proof that the tiny house is built properly. Many building departments validate this by automatically approving a tiny house on wheels with a certification from NOAH or RVIA. A second and typically more applicable way is to require the building plans and any documentation of the tiny house to be submitted to the building department.

Since the building department will require building plans and documentation of components such as the electrical installation, you must be methodical when purchasing a tiny house or having one built for you. Make sure that they have and will provide the architectural plans for you to submit to your local government. If you buy a tiny house or have one built that lacks documentation, don't expect the local government to approve it. Perhaps more importantly, don't blindly trust that a tiny house is safe just because someone else already lived in it or a contractor built it. You need to do your due diligence during the purchase process of any new or used tiny house to ensure that the sale is legitimate and the house is built properly.

When purchasing a prebuilt tiny house, ensure you have a clear title, as we covered during the land purchase section. If your tiny house on wheels is legally an RV, run the Vehicle Identification Number, or VIN, through the DMV and validate that it is registered.

The goal here is to ensure that you don't get scammed or oversold on your tiny house purchase, whether from a builder or a seller of a completed tiny house. Always take a buyer-beware mentality, enlist the help of a real estate agent or lawyer, and leave no stone unturned. It is okay to ask questions and do your due diligence. If a person or company is unwilling to cooperate, you don't want to work with them.

Is this really necessary?

It can be tempting to skip the building permit process and just build your tiny house out of sight and out of mind. The majority of people who take this route tend to avoid the zoning and planning departments entirely. No doubt, some people live undercover like this without issues, but there are a few major downsides.

The first and most significant is safety. Building permits are in place to ensure structures are safe even if the process feels overly bureaucratic, so skipping the permit process means you are assuming that your architectural plans are sound and your construction is precise. Second, suppose you skip the permit process, and your tiny house undergoes disaster, such as fire or flood damage. In that case, your tiny house insurance may not cover damages, assuming you can get insurance in the first place. Third, reselling your tiny house can be more challenging should you choose to resell one day; and fourth, if the building department discovers that you skipped the permit process, you will be required to get permits and pay fines.

While some people are willing to take these risks to save a few headaches and a few bucks, the seasoned builder would tell you to build your tiny house by the book to protect yourself from these risks.

Altogether, the process is not particularly complicated. It can be tedious, but you are just confirming your project with the local government before and after it is complete. Much like when we covered zoning, the build process encourages you to collaborate with the local building department.

BUILDING CODES

Now that you understand how the permit process works, it is time to unpack the topic of building codes. Building codes will affect construction but also the design itself. As a refresher from earlier in the book, the building codes are in place to ensure safe construction and living. While we could have a philosophical debate about the right and wrong of building code, doing so does not help us achieve our goal of living in a tiny house. Instead, it is better to acknowledge that tiny houses have some challenges when it comes to building code, but that code is not an inherent evil meant to prevent you from living happily. It has its merits and its shortcomings, but understand that it primarily exists for safety purposes.

You will need to find and read the code to best understand it. In the United States, there is a database of codes, and your local building department can certainly point you in the right direction or provide you with their local version of the code if they have one. They may simply use the default national code, even though in the US, the state has the power to regulate the safety of buildings. In the United States, that is the 2018 International Building Code (IBC), which is determined by the International Code Council (ICC). In Canada, it is the National Building Code of Canada 2015. Australia has the Australian Building Codes Board. To find the code in your country, just google "building codes of [country]" and look for an official website.

What codes apply to me?

There are many different codes that may apply. At a minimum, your building department will require that you meet a building code, or more specifically, a residential code. In most places in the United States, this means meeting the IRC, the residential code for single-family homes. Note that your jurisdiction may have a modified code or its own code entirely. For example, at the time of publishing this book, Wisconsin has its own residential code, while the other 49 states, Washington DC, Puerto Rico, Guam, and the US Virgin Islands have adopted the IRC. Another example is the International Mechanical Code (IMC), which focuses on ventilation, heating, and air conditioning. Only California, Vermont, Maine, and Hawaii have not adopted it.

Additionally, some states and municipalities adopt code updates at different times. The code is updated every three years at the ICC-level, but the power to adopt the code is still left to the states. Some states pass that power to the local level. This situation means that, when publishing this book, some states operate on the codes from 2015, others from 2018, and others from 2021. Codes from each of these years are available on the ICC website.

You will likely need to meet a handful of codes. Under the US-based codes determined by the ICC, tiny house owners often must meet the International Fire Code (IFC) and the International Plumbing Code (IPC). Some other codes that may apply include:

- International Building Code (IBC)
- International Energy Conservation Code (IECC)
- International Private Sewage Disposal (IPSDC)
- International Mechanical Code (IMC)
- International Fuel Gas Code (IFGC)
- International Wildland-Urban Interface (IWUIC)
- International Existing Building Code (IEBC)
- International Property Maintenance Code (IPMC)
- ICC Performance Code (ICCPC)
- Intl Green Construction Code (IgCC)
- International Swimming Pool and Spa Code (ISPSC)

While this list may at first appear overwhelming, know that these codes are all coordinated and compatible with each other. They can be found on the ICC website: *codes.iccsafe.org.*

Additionally, these codes are created from industry-wide stakeholders, including code officials, trade associations, manufacturers, buildings, government entities, designers, advocacy groups, utility companies, and anyone that wishes to participate. This collaboration makes the codes not only relevant but also easily understood. The code is not written in legal jargon that a layperson cannot understand but in plain English. It requires that you understand construction terminology or are willing to research it when reading the code, but that is expected when dealing with construction. The point is: *you do not need to be an expert to read and understand the code.*

Within this wide-reaching set of codes, tiny house-specific code has improved immensely. Specifically, *Appendix Q: Tiny Houses* of the IRC relaxes the code for homes under 400 square feet as long as they are on a fixed foundation. This code does not apply to tiny homes on wheels yet, as of publishing this book, but advocacy groups are pushing for further adoption to address this mobile need.

Appendix Q is not particularly long and is easily digestible on the ICC website. You can find it by googling *"IRC Appendix Q"* or using the URL provided in the references section of this book. That said, Appendix Q focuses mostly on relaxing code for tiny houses so that tiny houses can comply with the code. Before the existence of Appendix Q, it was nearly impossible to build a tiny house within the scope of the IRC. Since Appendix Q reduces ceiling height minimums, addresses loft requirements, stair and ladder requirements, and specifies emergency egress, builders can properly build a tiny house to code.

What about tiny houses on wheels?

Although tiny houses on wheels are not a part of the IRC code, many states and municipalities are quite friendly to tiny houses on wheels. Depending on local tiny house needs, your tiny house on wheels may only require a special permit to build, meaning that the local zoning and building departments approve of the project and collaborate with you to determine what construction requirements will be.

In some cases, your tiny house on wheels may simply be treated as an RV or mobile home. In this case, you will likely need to adhere to RVIA or NOAH certifications, which, as previously mentioned, means having your tiny house built by an RVIA-certified builder or NOAH-certified builder. You can become a NOAH-certified builder before you build your tiny mobile home, but becoming an RVIA-certified builder is reserved for true manufacturers.

How do I approach building codes and permits?

Your first step in this process is to talk to your building or planning department. You need to ask them what codes apply to your tiny house project and how to access those codes while also asking them to explain the process for your project.

There are several times when codes matter, so be sure to consider them throughout the following stages of your tiny house journey:

1) Design

To receive your building permits, your designs will need to be approved and, therefore, up to code. Designing the house from an aesthetic perspective is fun, but focusing on code is equally important. If you are designing your tiny house yourself, getting an architect to look at your plans before bringing them to the building department is advisable. If you are buying plans, make sure they meet the specific codes you need. One key reason that you want to be proactive with your code is that it shows the building department that you are doing things by the book, even though your house is a tiny house and a little out of the ordinary, which in turn may invite less scrutiny.

2) Approval

Once you have purchased or acquired your land, you will need to get formal approval and the permits themselves. Note that this is when you take your design to the building and possibly zoning departments to receive your permits. Special permits will be required in many places that allow tiny houses, so the design and approval steps may be somewhat iterative. You may need a variance from the standard code when receiving special permits. For example, your tiny house may not meet minimum size requirements, but the building department is still ok with you building your tiny house as planned. To get their official approval, you will need to apply for and receive a variance.

3) Construction

After formally receiving your permits, which is the local government's approval that your plans are to code, you must follow through on building to code. You may have an inspector show up at your construction site unannounced or have a checkpoint or two where the inspector comes to validate that construction is going as planned from a code perspective.

4) Inspection

You may or may not have inspections during construction, but you will definitely have them when the tiny house is complete. The inspector will sign off on your tiny house, and you will have a legitimately built tiny house on legitimately zoned land. It is important to document all steps of the build with photographs in case the inspector has any questions. For example, if the inspector asks about the location of the electrical rough-in, you need to make sure you can prove the answer to your question. Documenting the build is a good practice anyway, as it helps with reselling the house, insurance claims, and future renovations.

How do I read code?

As mentioned earlier, code is not intentionally confusing nor extremely filled with jargon, but it can take some time to get used to. When looking at code, you need to be patient and diligent.

Let's look at an example of code directly from the IRC:

AQ104.2.1.5 Handrails. *Handrails shall comply with Section R311.7.8.* This code is straight from Appendix Q in the IRC and tells you to refer to a different section. The R3 at the front of this code correlates to Chapter 3 of the code, so you must then refer to that Chapter and look for Code R311.7.8, which covers the requirements for handrails and says, *"Handrails shall be provided on not less than one side of each flight of stairs with four or more risers."* Breaking all of this down, Appendix Q tells us that handrails in a tiny house are required like in a normal house, meaning that you must have a handrail if you have four or more steps.

In addition to cross-referencing code, you will also come across many different acronyms, including but not limited to UL, ASTM, ANSI, NFPA, ASCE, and FEMA. Whenever you see one of these unknown acronyms, look it up. In many cases, it is an industry-specific safety standard, product validation, or reference to another specific code. Don't let these acronyms scare you; while you may not know what it is at first, a couple of minutes of researching it will solve your problem.

PERMITTING CHECKLIST

The permitting process is vital because it is the local government's stamp of approval for you to start construction. Within the permitting process, a handful of actions need to be completed.

1) Land Use

While at first you will likely talk to your zoning board and building department back and forth, land use and zoning verification need to be completed before applying for permits.

2) Prerequisites

Receive any prerequisite approvals. You may need approval from the fire, sewer, or water departments. For those putting in a septic system, you will likely need a soil report and a septic system permit. For those connecting to the municipal sewer, you will likely need a sewer permit. While all these approvals and permits can seem overwhelming, know that your contact at the local planning and building department can help guide you.

3) *Complete Plans*

Next, you will have to provide the complete plans. These plans must be drawn to scale and conform to local code. The building department may have other needs as well. In essence, the plans are a way for the building department to know what they are being asked to approve. Unless you have experience creating plans or are willing to learn how to use architectural design software, you should expect to buy the complete plans from a manufacturer or architect.

The first type of plan to consider is the site plan, which covers the house's location on the property and all of the important functions of the plot itself. Expect to include:

- Setback dimensions (which indicate where on the property the tiny house and structures like driveways will be placed in relation to the property boundaries. The zoning department will have setbacks outlined in the ordinance.)
- Easements
- Structural footprint, including structures like decks, and any existing structures on site already

- Location of water well
- Location of the septic tank
- Utility locations
- Lot area, building coverage area, and percentage of coverage (which is building coverage divided by lot area)
- Impervious area (which are areas that are highly resistant to water absorption, like driveways and rooftops)
- Surface drainage
- Greywater and blackwater plans
- Homesteading plans (such as creating a root cellar)

You may also need to include a foundation plan. Within a foundation plan, expect to include:

- Foundation dimensions
- Footings, columns, piers, and composition of foundation
- Locations and sizes of windows and doors
- Room sizes
- Heating appliances
- Exterior walls
- Plumbing location
- Smoke alarm
- Wood stove location

- Drains & Sump (if applicable)
- Connection details
- Vent size and location
- Connection details

Additionally, you will need to provide floor plans themselves, which will overlap with the other plans somewhat. Expect to include:

- Dimensions
- Room names
- Window and door sizes and locations
- Smoke detector location
- Water heaters and furnace locations
- Ventilation locations
- Plumbing locations
- Balconies and decks
- External structures

Beyond these plans, you will also need to submit plans for the floor, wall, and roof assemblies. You will also need to provide elevation views, which are sketches of what the house will look like when finished. Additionally, an electrical plan will be required, and any materials used will need to be outlined. You may also need to provide energy code compliance notes and depictions, engineer's calculations, and a radon mitigation plan.

Essentially, the building department wants to know exactly where the tiny house will be placed, what it will look like, and how it will be built. There is a reason that creating plans is a full-time profession for architects; it takes a lot of work and expertise to create! Luckily, the building department will help you understand what you need to provide them.

THE BUILDER'S MINDSET

Much like finding and buying land, construction requires diligence, patience, and perseverance. It also requires you to ask for help when needed and collaborate with your local government offices.

When thinking holistically about the building process, it is hard to deny that it is a bit drawn out and bureaucratic. But when we think about *why* the approach is this way, we can see that permitting and building codes are primarily in place for the safety of the tiny house and the safe treatment of the land it's on. So whether you find building codes and permitting to be reasonable or you find them to be overreaching and unjust, never forget the importance of safety. Building a potentially unsafe structure is simply a waste.

Give yourself time. Be meticulous. Ask for help where you need it. Work with the building department and your architect or manufacturer.

Remember why you want a tiny house, and let that motivation drive you. You got this; you are almost there!

FINAL WORDS

Dear Reader,

I hope this book has helped you. If nothing else, I hope it revealed that *building* a tiny house is only a fraction of what it takes to *live* in a tiny house.

Congratulations on making it to this point. Much of this book's content reveals just how challenging living legally in a tiny house can be, and I understand that this can feel overwhelming. Undoubtedly, some people will have read this book and realized they don't want to go through this effort. Others will have read this book and realized that they are willing to go through some of this effort but are willing to take a risk by circumventing some of it. A third group will have read this book and feel compelled to begin their journey to a fully legal tiny house. Whichever group you fall into, knowing just what steps must be taken is half the battle.

If you have the means and desire to live legally in a tiny house, you will have some difficulties to face. That said, they are relatively short-term, and you will overcome them with patience and diligence. Facing those difficulties now will establish a much stabler future for you, your family, and generations to come.

If you do not have the means or desire to follow the process in this book entirely, you also have some decisions to make. Ask yourself: *what steps am I willing to skip, and what risks must I accept by skipping them?* Ultimately, it is a personal choice. For many tiny house owners, doing things completely by the book simply never was an option due to its cost or the circumstances of their location or local government. If you go this route and go completely rogue, at least make sure you still build a safe home.

For all readers, you may be wondering what to do next. I encourage you to go back through the table of contents of this book and refer to each section as you begin the process from the top. This starts with identifying the fundamental reasons behind your desire for a tiny house. Once you have placed your motivation, get your finances in order without applying wishful thinking to your budget.

It is only at this point that you can start the land-buying process. Remember that finding land requires diligence, creativity, perseverance, patience, and good relationships with the local governments. Apply these principles, and you will, in time, find the right parcel of land. Once you find that parcel, you can continue with the code and construction process.

Finally, have fun with this as much as you can. Treat it as an adventure. Many tiny house owners say that the process of turning their tiny house dream into a functioning home was worthwhile. Some even go as far as to say the process was a transformation of their life in and of itself, that setting out to achieve an ambitious goal and actually achieving it made them a better version of themselves.

You, too, can achieve your goal and find that transformation.

To help you achieve this, I have created the **Tiny House Quickstarter**, a tool that helps you structure your budget, identify land opportunities, and a checklist of the steps needed in the tiny house process. You can sign up for it by joining the mailing list at **TinyHousePractical.com**.

If you enjoyed this book, I would be thrilled—and incredibly grateful—if you left a review on whichever platform you purchased it.

I wish you immense success on your tiny house journey!

Thanks again,

Jordan

OTHER BOOKS IN THIS SERIES

Scan the QR code to get it now!

Scan the QR code to get it now!

A HELPFUL TOOL FOR YOUR SUCCESS...

The supplemental **Tiny House Quickstarter** provides a tiny house checklist, a budgeting tool, a location tracker, and a list of must-avoid mistakes most people don't know they're making. Get yours now by going to my website!

Scan the QR code below!

jordanliberata.com

RESOURCES

INTRODUCTION

Liberata, J. (2021). *What is Your Biggest Tiny House Challenge?* [Dataset]. https://www.facebook.com/groups/tinyhouseconcepts/

CHAPTER 1

Broker vs. Realtor vs. Real Estate Agent. (2022, October 29). Investopedia. https://www.investopedia.com/ask/answers/101314/what-are-differences-among-real-estate-agent-broker-and-realtor.asp

Buying Land: How To Work Effectively WIth Real Estate Agents. (2019, January 21). Building Advisor. Retrieved June 1, 2022, from https://buildingadvisor.com/buying-land/making-an-offer/working-with-real-estate-agents/

Homepage | RVIA. (n.d.). https://www.rvia.org/

Liberata, J. (n.d.). *Live Tiny & Be Free: Everything You Need To Know About Tiny House Basics, Living, Ideas, and Design.* Troy Makes Books.

Liberata, J. (2022). *How to Build a Tiny House on Wheels Step by Step: Tiny Home Construction, Building, Plans, & Design.* Troy Makes Books.

CHAPTER 2

Akin, J. (2021, August 24). *What Is a USDA Loan?* Experian. https://www.experian.com/blogs/ask-experian/what-is-a-usda-loan/

Bank Rate. (n.d.). *Best Home Equity Loan Rates In January 2023.* Bankrate. https://www.bankrate.com/home-equity/home-equity-loan-rates/

Bell, L., & Bundrick, H. C. M. (2022a, July 3). *How Construction Loans Help Finance Your Dream House*. NerdWallet. https://www.nerdwallet.com/article/mortgages/construction-loans

Bringing Utilities to Vacant Land in 2023: 11 Things You Must Know. (2022, October 11). Gokce Capital: We Buy and Sell Land. https://gokce capital.com/bringing-utilities-to-land/

DiLallo, M. (2022, September 21). *How to Invest in Real Estate: A Complete Guide*. The Motley Fool. https://www.fool.com/investing/stock-market/market-sectors/real-estate-investing/

Home Services Expert. (2021, September 22). *What is Involved in the Permit Process when Building a House?* https://blog.expertsinyourhome.com/what-is-involved-in-the-permit-process-when-building-a-house

HomeGuide Editors. (2021a, August 18). *How much does a gravel driveway cost?* HomeGuide. https://homeguide.com/costs/gravel-driveway-cost

HomeGuide Editors. (2021b, August 28). *How Much Does It Cost To Drill Or Dig A Well?* HomeGuide. https://homeguide.com/costs/well-drilling-cost

How to Apply for a Personal Loan. (2022, July 22). Investopedia. https://www.investopedia.com/articles/personal-finance/010516/how-apply-personal-loan.asp

How to Get Tiny House Financing. (2021, July 7). US News. https://loans.usnews.com/articles/how-to-get-tiny-house-financing

Joining the RVIA | American Tiny House Association. (n.d.). https://americantinyhouseassociation.org/joining-the-rvia/

Kasch, A. (2022, October 11). *How Much Does a Gravel Driveway Cost?* Angi. https://www.angi.com/articles/how-much-does-gravel-driveway-cost.htm

Land Century. (2018a, February 26). *Bringing Utilities to an Undeveloped Plot of Land - What to Expect*. https://www.landcentury.com/articles-news/bringing-utilities-to-an-undeveloped-plot-of-land-what-to-expect

Land Century. (2018b, February 26). *Bringing Utilities to an Undeveloped Plot of Land - What to Expect.* https://www.landcentury.com/articles-news/bringing-utilities-to-an-undeveloped-plot-of-land-what-to-expect

Landscapes, C. (2021, September 3). *How To Prepare Your Property For Drainage.* Couvillion's Landscapes. https://www.couvillionslandscaping.com/how-to-prepare-your-property-for-drainage/

Learn how much it costs to Hire an Architect. (n.d.). https://www.homeadvisor.com/cost/architects-and-engineers/hire-an-architect/

Learn how much it costs to Install a Water Treatment & Purification System - Compose: SEO. (n.d.). https://www.homeadvisor.com/cost/environmental-safety/install-a-water-treatment-and-purification-system/

Learn how much it costs to Install Drainage. (n.d.). https://www.homeadvisor.com/cost/landscape/install-drainage/

Learn how much it costs to Run a Perc Test - Compose: SEO. (n.d.). https://www.homeadvisor.com/cost/architects-and-engineers/perc-soil-test/

Marquit, M. (2022, September 23). *What are construction loans, and how do they work?* Bankrate. https://www.bankrate.com/mortgages/construction-loans-explained/

Martin, E. J. (2020, October 22). *How home construction loans work.* Mortgage Rates, Mortgage News and Strategy: The Mortgage Reports. https://themortgagereports.com/65876/how-home-construction-loans-work

Millerbernd, A., & Choudhuri-Wade, R. (2023, January 5). *What Credit Score Do You Need for a Personal Loan?* NerdWallet. https://www.nerdwallet.com/article/loans/personal-loans/credit-score-need-get-personal-loan

Mobile Home Insurance: Do You Need It? (2022, January 28). Investopedia. https://www.investopedia.com/mobile-home-insurance-do-you-need-it-5073075

Morneau, P. B. D., Morneau, P. B. D., & Morneau, P. B. D. (n.d.). *How to Find Land for Tiny Houses?* Tiny House Society. https://www.tinysociety.co/articles/how-to-find-land-for-tiny-houses/

Named Perils Insurance Policy. (2022, March 25). Investopedia. https://www.investopedia.com/terms/n/named_perils.asp

NOAH RDI | MEMBERSHIP PAGE. (n.d.). https://noahcertified.org/membership-page/

Perc Testing and Soil Testing - What You Need to Know. (2022, May 15). Building Advisor. https://buildingadvisor.com/buying-land/septic-systems/soil-and-perc-testing/

Personal Loan Calculator. (2023, January 19). NerdWallet. https://www.nerdwallet.com/article/loans/personal-loans/personal-loan-calculator

Pricing Guide: How Much Does It Cost to Clear Land? (2022, December 2). Lawnstarter. https://www.lawnstarter.com/blog/cost/clear-land-price/

Real Estate Lawyer Fees. (2022, April 2). Thumbtack. https://www.thumbtack.com/p/real-estate-lawyer-fees

SBA 504 Loans. (n.d.). SBA. https://www.sba.gov/funding-programs/loans/504-loans

The Best Tiny House Insurance in 2023. (2022, November 27). Investopedia. https://www.investopedia.com/best-tiny-house-insurance-5120510

Tiny House Insurance: How to Insure Your Tiny Home. (2021, March 4). Investopedia. https://www.investopedia.com/tiny-house-insurance-how-to-insure-your-tiny-home-5074333

Tomsich, E. (2023a, January 11). *Land Loans: Everything You Need To Know*. Rocket Mortgage. https://www.rocketmortgage.com/learn/land-loans

Vacant Land Loan Calculator: 100% Financing Property Purchase Payment Calculator. (n.d.). https://www.mortgagecalculator.org/calcs/land.php

Valzania, M. (2018, January 29). *Off The Grid Living Part Three: Waste*. LandCentral. https://blog.landcentral.com/land-university-blog/grid-living-part-three-waste/

Vandenboss, K. (2023, January 19). *What Is a Land Survey, and When Do You Need One?* The Motley Fool. https://www.fool.com/investing/stock-market/market-sectors/real-estate-investing/basics/land-survey-cost/

What are Impact Fees? 13 Things (2022) You Need to Know. (2022, July 17). Gokce Capital: We Buy and Sell Land. https://gokcecapital.com/impact-fees/

Why Choose an Insurance Broker Over an Insurance Agent? (n.d.). https://www.howdengroup.com/sg-en/why-choose-insurance-broker-over-insurance-agent

Wichter, Z. (2022, December 21). *What property buyers should know about land loans.* Bankrate. https://www.bankrate.com/mortgages/what-property-buyers-should-know-about-land-loans/

Womeldorf, R. (2022, February 19). *How Much Does It Cost to Set Up Utilities on Land?* Upgraded Home. https://upgradedhome.com/how-much-does-it-cost-to-set-up-utilities-on-land/

CHAPTER 3

11Th, B. 2. R. P. ·. A. (n.d.). *Tiny House Statistics (2022): Market Size & Industry Growth.* https://www.getonedesk.com/tiny-house-statistics

Avallone Law Associates. (2019, December 16). *Zoning ordinance violations and penalties in Pennsylvania.* https://www.lawrenceavallone.com/blog/2018/09/zoning-ordinance-violations-and-penalties-in-pennsylvania/

Centers, J. (2017, May 18). *How to Ensure High-speed Internet Access When Buying a New Home.* TidBITS. https://tidbits.com/2017/05/18/how-to-ensure-high-speed-internet-access-when-buying-a-new-home/

FEMA Flood Map Service Center | Welcome! (n.d.). https://msc.fema.gov/portal/home

Hendrix, J. M. (2022, November 29). *Real estate land use and property types.* LandSearch. https://www.landsearch.com/blog/land-use-types-definitions

In a Bid to Speed Development, Britain Gives Zoning a Try. (2020, August 13). Bloomberg. https://www.bloomberg.com/news/articles/2020-08-13/britain-proposes-radical-overhaul-of-city-planning#:~:text=Under%20the%20current%20system%2C%20introduced,use%20on%20already%20developed%20sites

Kai Andrew. (2021, April 6). *Single Mom Making $50K/MONTH From A $315k Property* [Video]. YouTube. https://www.youtube.com/watch?v=wAUmeLGL2ao

Morneau, P. B. D., Morneau, P. B. D., & Morneau, P. B. D. (n.d.). *How to Find Land for Tiny Houses?* Tiny House Society. https://www.tinysociety.co/articles/how-to-find-land-for-tiny-houses/

Olson, S. A. (2017, October 5). *Rural Internet Options: How to Connect in the Country*. rethinkrural.raydientplaces.com. https://rethinkrural.raydientplaces.com/blog/rural-internet-options-how-to-connect-in-the-country

randymajors.org Research Hub. (2022, December 29). *County Lines*. https://www.randymajors.org/countygmap

Ross, B. (2015, July 21). *Who Owns the Minerals Under Your Property*. www.nolo.com. https://www.nolo.com/legal-encyclopedia/who-owns-the-minerals-under-your-property.html

Russell, R. (2021, December 16). *The Process for Buying Land with Cash in 11 Simple Steps*. HomeLight Blog. https://www.homelight.com/blog/buyer-process-for-buying-land-with-cash/

Samuel, A. (2020, June 4). *Dont Drill A Well Until You Read This*. Vacant Land USA. https://vacantland-usa.com/drill-a-well/

Steve Sanders at LotNetwork.com. (2020, October 23). *Utilities & Infrastructure Tips When Buying Lots & Land - LotNetwork.com*. LotNetwork.com Blog. https://blog.lotnetwork.com/utilities-infrastructure-tip-5-for-buying-lots-and-land/

The A to Z of Land Uses: Understanding Land-Use Specifics. (2020, August 13). Land.com. https://network.land.com/buying/guide-to-land-use-definitions/

The FEMA 100 year flood zone explained. | MassiveCert - Massively Easy Flood Certification. (n.d.). https://www.massivecert.com/blog/fema-100-year-flood-zone-explained

Tiny House Zoning Crash Course. (2022, April 13). Tiny House Practical. https://www.tinyhousepractical.com/post/tiny-house-zoning-crash-course

What Is An Easement? Definition + Tips For Homeowners. (2022, November 21). https://www.quickenloans.com/learn/easement

Who Zones? Mapping Land-Use Authority across the US. (2019, December 9). [Video]. Urban Institute. https://www.urban.org/urban-wire/who-zones-mapping-land-use-authority-across-us

CHAPTER 4

12 tools for sleuthing real estate leads. (2015, July 29). Inman. https://www.inman.com/2015/07/29/12-tools-for-sleuthing-real-estate-leads-and-property-owners/

Albaum, M. (2022, June 6). *11 best ways to find off-market properties in 2022*. https://learn.roofstock.com/blog/off-market-properties

Auctions | Consumer Protection. (n.d.). https://www.consumerprotection.govt.nz/general-help/ways-to-buy-and-pay/auctions/

Beautiful, modern cabin design. (n.d.). https://land.nyc/guides/purchasing-land-a-due-diligence-checklist/

Buying a Home: 8 Disclosures Sellers Must Make. (2022, March 15). Investopedia. https://www.investopedia.com/articles/personal-finance/061214/real-estate-flipping-8-disclosures-you-must-make.asp

Co., D. B. L. T. (2019, June 20). *How do I find land for my tiny house? - #AskTheDreamTeam*. Dream Big Live Tiny Co. https://www.dreambiglivetinyco.com/blogs/askthedreamteam/how-do-i-find-land-for-my-tiny-house

Compagine-Cohen, A. (2022, November 9). *The Process for Buying Land with Cash*. UpNest. https://www.upnest.com/1/post/10-easy-steps-for-buying-land-with-cash/

Deeds.com. (2020, October 14). *Transferring a Deed Without a Lawyer? Here's What You Should Know*. https://www.deeds.com/articles/transferring-a-deed-without-a-lawyer-heres-what-you-should-know/

Esajian, J. D. (2022, July 27). *Blog.* FortuneBuilders. https://www.fortunebuilders.com/real-estate-auction-process/

Fawcett, D. C. (2019, December 18). *Four Ways To Find Off-Market Properties For Sale.* Forbes. https://www.forbes.com/sites/forbesrealestatecouncil/2019/12/18/four-ways-to-find-off-market-properties-for-sale/?sh=8a90ec5626c6

Fitzgerald, J. (2022a, July 25). *How to Buy Land: A Step-by-Step Guide.* Family Handyman. https://www.familyhandyman.com/article/how-to-buy-land/

How To Find Out Who Owns A Property. (2023, January 5). Quicken Loans. https://www.quickenloans.com/learn/how-to-find-out-who-owns-a-property

Learn About Buying a Short Sale or Waiting for a Foreclosure. (2021, July 19). The Balance. https://www.thebalancemoney.com:443/short-sale-or-foreclosure-1799094

Learn how much it costs to Hire a Home Appraiser - Compose: SEO. (n.d.). https://www.homeadvisor.com/cost/inspectors-and-appraisers/hire-a-property-appraiser/

Multivista. (2021, November 25). *A Due Diligence Checklist for Real Estate Development.* https://www.multivista.com/blog/a-due-diligence-checklist-for-real-estate-development/

NAEBA. (2019, August 29). *What Exactly are Buyer's Agent Responsibilities?* https://naeba.org/what-exactly-are-the-responsibilities-of-a-buyer-agent/

Nolo. (2015, September 22). *Judgment Liens on Property in Pennsylvania.* www.nolo.com. https://www.nolo.com/legal-encyclopedia/judgment-liens-pennsylvania-46854.html

Rate, G. (2023, January 23). *What Is a Property Title Search?* https://www.rate.com/resources/what-is-title-search

Ross, B. (2014, March 26). *Before Buying Vacant Land: Getting an Environmental Assessment.* www.nolo.com. https://www.nolo.com/legal-encyclopedia/before-buying-vacant-land-getting-environmental-assessment.html

Russell, R. (2021, December 16). *The Process for Buying Land with Cash in 11 Simple Steps*. HomeLight Blog. https://www.homelight.com/blog/buyer-process-for-buying-land-with-cash/

Seltzer, C. (2016a, November 22). *13 Documents You Should Have Before Buying Country Property*. LANDTHINK. https://www.landthink.com/13-documents-you-should-have-before-buying-country-property/

Seltzer, C. (2016b, November 22). *13 Documents You Should Have Before Buying Country Property*. LANDTHINK. https://www.landthink.com/13-documents-you-should-have-before-buying-country-property/

State Disclosure Laws. (n.d.). www.nolo.com. https://www.nolo.com/legal-encyclopedia/state-state-seller-disclosure-requirements

Steve Sanders at LotNetwork.com. (2020, May 20). *How to Buy Land at Auction: Benefits and Terms for Buyers*. LotNetwork.com Blog. https://blog.lotnetwork.com/buy-land-auction/

Tax Sale: Definition, How It Works, Two Types. (2022a, May 10). Investopedia. https://www.investopedia.com/terms/t/tax-sale.asp

Tiny House Basics. (2021, March 12). *Find Land NOW For Your Tiny House!* https://www.tinyhousebasics.com/find-land-now-for-your-tiny-house/

Title Search: What It Is, How It's Done, and Title Insurance. (2022, April 23). Investopedia. https://www.investopedia.com/terms/t/titlesearch.asp

Toebe, C. (2021, May 6). *How to Buy Raw Land: A 4-Part Guide to Making the Right Choices*. wikiHow. https://www.wikihow.com/Buy-Raw-Land

Understanding Escrow. (2022, June 13). Investopedia. https://www.investopedia.com/mortgage/escrow-process-requirements/

What Does A Title Company Do? (2022, December 7). Quicken Loans. https://www.quickenloans.com/learn/what-does-a-title-insurance-company-do

Williams, S. (n.d.). *How to Close a Cash Land Transaction In-House (Full DIY Instructions!)*. REtipster. https://retipster.com/how-to-close-cash-transaction/

CHAPTER 5

Contributor, T. (2019, August 1). *Appendix Q: Tiny Houses On A Foundation*. Tiny Home Industry Association. https://tinyhomeindustryas sociation.org/appendix-q-tiny-houses-on-a-foundation/

Home Services Expert. (2021, September 22). *What is Involved in the Permit Process when Building a House?* https://blog.expertsiny ourhome.com/what-is-involved-in-the-permit-process-when-building-a-house

ICC Code Adoption Maps. (n.d.). ICC. https://www.iccsafe.org/wp-content/uploads/Code_Adoption_Maps.pdf

ICCMEDIA. (2011a, July 6). *Building Codes 101, Part II: ICC and Building Codes* [Video]. YouTube. https://www.youtube.com/watch?v= 7BeU64RHW7A

ICCMEDIA. (2011b, August 10). *Building Codes 101, Part I: Introduction to Building Codes* [Video]. YouTube. https://www.youtube.com/ watch?v=Kk358ZZa8pk

Impervious Coverage Definition. (n.d.). Law Insider. https://www.lawin sider.com/dictionary/impervious-coverage

International Code Council (ICC). (n.d.-a). *2018 INTERNATIONAL RESIDENTIAL CODE (IRC) | ICC DIGITAL CODES*. https://codes. iccsafe.org/content/IRC2018/appendix-q-tiny-houses

International Code Council (ICC). (n.d.-b). *Find Codes*. https://codes. iccsafe.org/codes/i-codes

LandCentral. (2018, July 31). *Property Setbacks: What Are They and Why Do They Matter?* https://blog.landcentral.com/land-university-blog/ property-setbacks-what-are-they-and-why-do-they-matter/

Planning Drawings: Here's What Architects Say About Planning Drawings | Urbanist Architecture - London Architects. (n.d.). Urbanist Architecture. https://urbanistarchitecture.co.uk/planning-drawings/

Understanding the Construction Permit Process. (2022, February 23). The Spruce. https://www.thespruce.com/what-is-a-building-permit-1398344

What are Foundation Plan Drawings and Why Do You Need Them for Construction Projects? (2022, December 12). BluEnt Engineering. https://www.bluentcad.com/blog/foundation-plan-drawing/

Made in the USA
Middletown, DE
12 December 2024

66890775R00111